Food Culture in South America

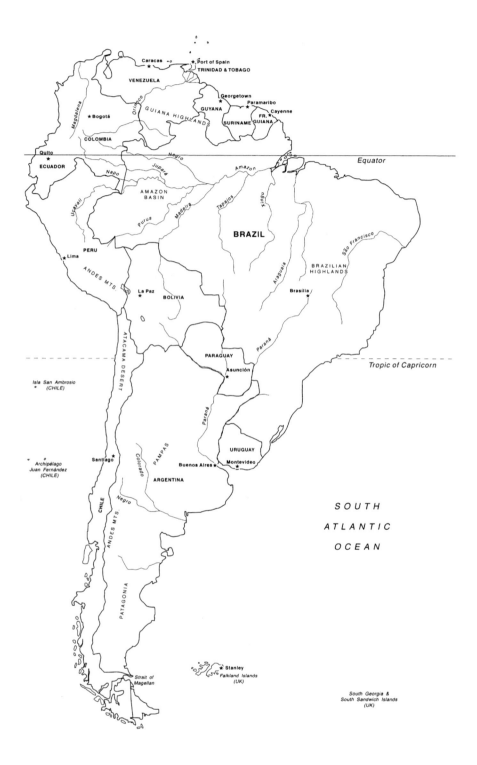

Caracas ★ ‑o

★ Port of Spain
TRINIDAD & TOBAGO

VENEZUELA

Georgetown
★
Paramaribo
★
Cayenne
FR. ★
GUIANA

GUYANA

SURINAME

GUIANA HIGHLANDS

Orinoco

Magdalena

★ Bogotá

COLOMBIA

Quito
★
ECUADOR

Equator

Negro

Napo

Japurá

Amazon

Ucayali

AMAZON
BASIN

Purus

Madeira

Tapajos

Xingu

BRAZIL

PERU

★ Lima

ANDES MTS.

La Paz
★
BOLIVIA

São Francisco

BRAZILIAN
HIGHLANDS

Araguaia

Brasília
★

ATACAMA DESERT

Isla San Ambrosio
o
(CHILE)

Tropic of Capricorn

PARAGUAY

Paraná

Asunción
★

Archipélago
Juan Fernández
(CHILE)

Santiago
★

Colorado

PAMPAS

Parana

Buenos Aires ★

Montevideo
★

URUGUAY

ARGENTINA

CHILE

Negro

ANDES MTS.

SOUTH

ATLANTIC

OCEAN

PATAGONIA

Strait of
Magellan

★ Stanley
Falkland Islands
(UK)

South Georgia &
South Sandwich Islands
(UK)

Food Culture in
South America

JOSÉ RAFAEL LOVERA

Translated by Ainoa Larrauri

Food Culture around the World
Ken Albala, Series Editor

GREENWOOD PRESS
Westport, Connecticut · London

Library of Congress Cataloging-in-Publication Data

Lovera, José Rafael.
    Food culture in South America / José Rafael Lovera ; translated by Ainoa Larrauri.
      p. cm. — (Food culture around the world, ISSN 1545–2638)
    Includes bibliographical references and index.
    ISBN 0–313–32752–1 (alk. paper)
    1. Cookery, Latin American. 2. Cookery—South America. 3. Food habits—South
America. I. Title. II. Series.
TX716.A1L68   2005
641.598—dc22   2005005501

British Library Cataloguing in Publication Data is available.

Library of Congress Catalog Card Number: 2005005501
ISBN: 0–313–32752–1
ISSN: 1545–2638

First published in 2005

Greenwood Press, 88 Post Road West, Westport, CT 06881
An imprint of Greenwood Publishing Group, Inc.
www.greenwood.com

Printed in the United States of America

The paper used in this book complies with the
Permanent Paper Standard issued by the National
Information Standards Organization (Z39.48–1984).

10 9 8 7 6 5 4 3 2 1

Illustrations by J. Susan Cole Stone.

The publisher has done its best to make sure the instructions and/or recipes in this book
are correct. However, users should apply judgment and experience when preparing recipes, especially parents and teachers working with young people. The publisher accepts no
responsibility for the outcome of any recipe included in this volume.

Contents

Series Foreword

The appearance of the Food Culture around the World series marks a definitive stage in the maturation of Food Studies as a discipline to reach a wider audience of students, general readers, and foodies alike. In comprehensive interdisciplinary reference volumes, each on the food culture of a country or region for which information is most in demand, a remarkable team of experts from around the world offers a deeper understanding and appreciation of the role of food in shaping human culture for a whole new generation. I am honored to have been associated with this project as series editor.

Each volume follows a series format, with a chronology of food-related dates and narrative chapters entitled Introduction, Historical Overview, Major Foods and Ingredients, Cooking, Typical Meals, Eating Out, Special Occasions, and Diet and Health. Each also includes a glossary, bibliography, resource guide, and illustrations.

Finding or growing food has of course been the major preoccupation of our species throughout history, but how various peoples around the world learn to exploit their natural resources, come to esteem or shun specific foods and develop unique cuisines reveals much more about what it is to be human. There is perhaps no better way to understand a culture, its values, preoccupations and fears, than by examining its attitudes toward food. Food provides the daily sustenance around which families and communities bond. It provides the material basis for rituals through which people celebrate the passage of life stages and their connection to divinity.

Food preferences also serve to separate individuals and groups from each other, and as one of the most powerful factors in the construction of identity, we physically, emotionally and spiritually become what we eat.

By studying the foodways of people different from ourselves we also grow to understand and tolerate the rich diversity of practices around the world. What seems strange or frightening among other people becomes perfectly rational when set in context. It is my hope that readers will gain from these volumes not only an aesthetic appreciation for the glories of the many culinary traditions described, but also ultimately a more profound respect for the peoples who devised them. Whether it is eating New Year's dumplings in China, folding tamales with friends in Mexico or going out to a famous Michelin-starred restaurant in France, understanding these food traditions helps us to understand the people themselves.

As globalization proceeds apace in the twenty-first century it is also more important than ever to preserve unique local and regional traditions. In many cases these books describe ways of eating that have already begun to disappear or have been seriously transformed by modernity. To know how and why these losses occur today also enables us to decide what traditions, whether from our own heritage or that of others, we wish to keep alive. These books are thus not only about the food and culture of peoples around the world, but also about ourselves and who we hope to be.

Ken Albala
University of the Pacific

Acknowledgments

Writing this book has been a challenge and a pleasure at the same time. A challenge, because great efforts were necessary to compress the vast information represented by the food culture of more than 12 countries. And a pleasure, because for years I have been dedicated to the study of this topic and because, as a South American, I am pleased to be given the opportunity to spread this culture in the United States. Many people have made contributions to this book. It would be impossible to mention them all, but I want to refer to some of them either by name or in a general way, to all of whom I express my most sincere gratitude. Both the editor of this series, Ken Albala, and the acquisitions editor of Greenwood Press, Wendi Schnaufer, not only allowed me to be the author of this book, but also patiently read each of the chapters, making suggestions and encouraging me constantly throughout the work. I particularly want to express my profound appreciation for the contribution of the numerous friends—experts on the gastronomy of the different South American countries—who have conversed with me during the journeys I have undertaken for a number of years to the different zones of the continent. I must also express my gratitude to two persons who worked as my research assistants, namely Cordelia Arias Toledo and Marilyn Sivira, who were also involved in the transcription of the manuscript. Similarly, I need to mention Ainoa Larrauri, whom I hired to translate the manuscript—a task she performed to my satisfaction. I had fruitful long talks with her aimed at guaranteeing that the English version accurately expressed my ideas and the information I had gathered. I also want to thank Graciela Valery de Vélez, among other people, for help with recipes. I hope I have fulfilled the objective of spreading the South American food culture, while I assume the entire responsibility for any possible defects of my work.

Introduction

Giving a detailed account of South American food culture is a challenging task. This continent comprises more than 10 countries, its inhabitants do not all speak the same language, and the food traditions of the different societies vary in some ways. People's diets are not only the result of certain traditions—cultural heritage, cooking techniques, and so on—but they are also strongly related to the geographical environment. The vast South American continent can roughly be divided into four large zones, taking into consideration geographical and cultural characteristics: the Andes, the Llanos and Pampas, Amazonia, and the coastal areas.

The Andean region starts from western Venezuela and runs in a southerly direction along Colombia, Ecuador, Peru, Bolivia, Chile, and Argentina, down to Tierra del Fuego. The Andes can be considered South America's backbone. They feature a great number of mountains, plateaus, hillsides, and valleys. Countless rivers run from their highlands, while perennial snows cover their summits. Almost all climates can be found in this elongated region, from hot to cold. It was the cradle of the only urban cultures that existed in the region in pre-Hispanic times and, traditionally, the place where the largest number of inhabitants would settle. Headquarters of the most developed agricultural systems in ancient South America, the Andes are the birthplace of the potato, which is a staple food of the continent, and the place where corn and beans were grown—two key foods that were never totally displaced despite the transculturation process that took place with the arrival of the Europeans.

The Llanos and Pampas zone not only refers to the Venezuelan and the Argentinean plains, but also includes, by extension, the Brazilian and Uruguayan ones, which can be put on an equal footing for the purposes of the general classification that is being proposed here, although they are not exactly equal. This zone features vast expanses of mostly plains—some of which were seabeds, according to geologists—stretching from the central region of Venezuela and running along northeastern Colombia, southern Brazil, Uruguay, and practically halfway through Argentina, between the Andes and the Atlantic coasts (from east to west) and between the Atlantic Ocean and Patagonia (from north to south). These vast plains have herbaceous vegetation and an average height of about 1,000 feet. The climate in the Venezuelan and Colombian Llanos is mostly hot, whereas that of the Pampas is temperate to continental. These regions were not peopled by sedentary tribes; neither were they home to any urban culture during pre-Hispanic times. With the arrival of the Europeans, cattle and horses were introduced in the New World and reproduced copiously in the Llanos and Pampas, to such an extent that their inhabitants—the *llaneros* and the gauchos—are typically regarded as stockbreeders.

Amazonia, in a very broad sense, stretches to the north and to the south of the equator and comprises the Guianas; southern Venezuela; southeastern Colombia; parts of Bolivia, Ecuador, Peru, and Paraguay; and the northern half of Brazil. It is characterized mainly by lowlands covered by forest and crossed by countless rivers, among which the most important are the Amazon and the Orinoco. The climate is predominantly tropical. The zone had been occupied by a few wandering tribes before the arrival of the Europeans and, even today, is the least populated area in South America. A typical foodstuff of this zone is cassava root, which is still a staple in the region.

The coastal zone, making up the continental perimeter and characterized by lands at sea level, can be divided into three subregions: the Atlantic coasts, which more or less stretch from the Guianas to Tierra del Fuego; the Caribbean coasts, which actually correspond to the borderline that runs from the mouth of the Orinoco River to Panama, but which for cultural reasons generally include the shores of the Guianas; and finally the Pacific coasts, which stretch from the borderline between Colombia and Panama to Tierra del Fuego. This coastal zone has a variable climate, but this is the area through which the Europeans entered the continent and therefore was the home of the first settlements they founded. As it is next to the sea, this zone has always profited from its bounty.

The arbitrary division here must only be taken as a guide that facilitates locating typical South American dishes and as a simplified form of what could be called a gastronomical map of South America. Gaining a clear picture of South American food culture requires first familiarizing oneself with the history of its people, who are the result of a strong biological and cultural mixing process that took place during the last 500 years. This process gave rise to a new society with particular foodways that include a mixture of the different cultures involved. Nowadays, the foods that were mainly used by the Indians still play an important role in the South American cuisine, though along with other foods that were brought by the successive immigrations that took place during those five centuries. It is particularly important to highlight that the South American region features dishes, cooking techniques, and thus food habits, which have played a role throughout history almost without modification for time immemorial. Therefore, historical references are of key importance—or, rather, are necessary for the understanding of a reality in which the past is still alive.

Historically regarded as a woman's work, food preparation is in recent times also performed by men. There are still two ways in which cooking can be considered: in rural parts, the practices of the colonial times are still in use; in urban areas, modernization brought about by urban sprawl and new cultural transfers has transformed cooking.

South Americans eat at least three times in a day. The mealtimes vary within the continent; there are differences among the countries. Dinner is perhaps the most important of the three meals. In any case, the dishes that are typical for each of these three occasions will be presented insofar as is possible.

Most meals are eaten at home, but there have been food vendors on the streets, in the markets, and even along the pathways since colonial times. During republican times, restaurants, cafés, and other public food stands began to appear, which led people—especially in a city—to spontaneously or by necessity start eating out more frequently.

South Americans celebrate a great number of both secular and religious events that involve food. For many of these celebrations, special dishes are served.

Regarding nutrition, South Americans preserve some ancient traditions from the pre-Columbian or the colonial times, but they also have up-to-date dietary knowledge—especially in the cities. Studies have been done on the calorie content of the typical diet of tropical lands, as well as on the nutritional values of the staple foods. In contemporary times, certain socioeconomic problems have brought about changes in the food habits, which have had important effects on the population's health.

Timeline

6000–3000 B.C.   Gourds (*Curcubita pepo*) are present in Peru.

5800 B.C.   Beans (*Phaseolus lunatus*) are present on the central coast of Peru.

5000 B.C.   Potatoes (*Solanum tuberosum*) are cultivated in the Andean zone.

4000 B.C.   Corn pollen is present in Ecuadorian Amazonia.

3000 B.C.   Corn (*Zea mays*) spreads from Central America to North and South America.

2500 B.C.   Algae is consumed in coastal Peru.

2000 B.C.   Peanuts (*Arachis hypogea* L.) are cultivated in Peru.

2000–1900 B.C.   Potatoes are cultivated in Peru. Perhaps they were domesticated in Venezuela by this time.

1400–900 B.C.   Cassava (*Manihot esculenta*) is cultivated in Colombia and Venezuela.

Corn is cultivated on the Pacific coast and the western mountain range of Ecuador and Peru, the eastern and central mountain range of Bolivia, and the northern mountain range of Argentina.

1000–900 B.C.   Potatoes are cultivated in Chile, Argentina, Bolivia, and Ecuador.

	Sweet potatoes (*Ipomoea batatas*) are cultivated in Venezuela, Colombia, Ecuador, and Peru.
700 B.C.	Aztecs and Incas are the first to be credited with trading and consuming of tomatoes.
600–500 B.C.	Squash (*Cucurbita maxima*) is present in Argentina.
500–600 A.D.	Cassava is domesticated in Guyana, Suriname, French Guiana, and Brazil.
600–700	Squash is present in northern Chile.
1400–1500	Terrace cultivation (*andenes*) is practiced in the Andean zone.
1498	Italian explorer Christopher Columbus catches sight of the South American coasts for the first time when he sails into the Gulf of Paria, between Venezuela and Trinidad.
1500–1600	Sorghum (*Sorghum vulgare*) from Africa is introduced to Brazil.
	Wheat (*Triticum* spp.) is cultivated in Venezuela, Colombia, Ecuador, Peru, Chile, Bolivia, Argentina, Uruguay, and Brazil.
	The cultivation of rice (*Oryza sativa*) begins in Venezuela, Brazil, and Bolivia.
	Bananas (*Musa* spp.) are domesticated in Colombia, Ecuador, Peru, Brazil, Paraguay, and Bolivia.
	Yams (*Dioscorea alata*), native to Africa, are brought to Brazil, Peru, Guyana, and Suriname along with the African slaves.
	Sugar cane (*Saccharum officinarum*) is cultivated in Venezuela, Colombia, Ecuador, Peru, Bolivia, and Argentina.
	Sweet potatoes are cultivated in Guyana, Suriname, French Guiana, Brazil, Paraguay, Uruguay, and Argentina.
1500	Expedition led by Portuguese navigator Pedro Álvarez Cabral reaches the coasts of Brazil.
1509	Spanish navigator Juan de la Cosa, sailing for Spain, arrives in Turbaco, Colombia.
1516	In February, Juan Díaz de Solís, a Spanish navigator, reaches the mouth of the River Plate in Argentina.
1519	Portuguese explorer Ferdinand Magellan catches sight of the coasts of Brazil, particularly the Cape of San Agustín.

1520	The Portuguese start producing sugar in Brazil.
1521	Brother Bartolomé de las Casas founds the first mission on the mainland, in Cumaná, Venezuela.
1524	Inca prince, Huayna Cápac, dies in Quito and his sons Huascar and Atahualpa start fighting each other for control of the empire.
1527	Spanish conqueror Juan de Ampíes founds the city of Coro in western Venezuela.
1532	Francisco Pizarro, a Spanish conqueror, finally arrives in Peru and manages to take control of the Inca Empire. Portuguese navigator Martim Afonso de Sousa establishes a colony in Brazil.
1542	The Viceroyalty of Peru is created.
1546	Francisco de Orellana carries out the Amazon River expedition.
1555	Andrés Laguna's work *Pedacio Dioscórides Anazarbeo, acerca de la materia medicinal y de los venenos mortíferos* (Pedacio Dioscórides Anazarbeo, Concerning Medicinal Material and Deadly Poisons), one of the most famous books on medicinal plant repertoires, is published in Antwerp, Belgium.
1569	Colonists in Brazil enjoy a diet largely based on the dish known as *feijoada completa*, a kind of cassoulet.
1590	The work *Historia natural y moral de las Indias* (The Natural and Moral History of the Indies) by Jesuit missionary José de Acosta is published in Seville, Spain.
1615	Cacao (*Thebroma cacao* L.) is first cultivated in coastal Venezuela.
1677	Cacao is cultivated in Brazil.
1700–1800	Planned cultivation of rye (*Secale cereale*) takes place in Brazil and Argentina.
	Oats (*Avena sativa*) are introduced by the Europeans to Colombia, Ecuador, Brazil, Chile, Paraguay, and Argentina.
1714	The Dutch bring coffee plants to Suriname.
1717	Viceroyalties of New Granada and Brazil are created.
1741	The existence of coffee in the province of Caracas (Venezuela) is pointed out.

1776   Viceroyalty of the River Plate is created.

1800–1900   In the early nineteenth century, the book *Cozinheiro Imperial ou Nova arte do cozinheiro e do copeiro em todos os seus ramos* (Imperial Cook, or the New Art of Cooks and Butlers in All of Their Fields) is published in Rio de Janeiro under the initials R.C.M., with a second edition in 1843.

1810   On April 19, a governing junta is installed in Caracas.

                On July 20, a Patriotic Junta is installed in Bogotá.

                The independence of Buenos Aires is proclaimed on May 25.

                In Santiago de Chile, independence from Spain is declared with the installation of the governing junta on September 18.

1811   On July 5, the Independence Declaration of Venezuela is signed.

1816   The Congress of Tucumán meets on July 19 and declares the independence of the United Provinces of the River Plate (now Argentina and Uruguay).

1818   In Venezuela, the German physician J.G.B. Siegert develops his *amargo de Angostura*, a beverage that improved digestive well-being and that was then used in cocktails.

                The Battle of Maipú allows for Chile's proclamation of independence with the victory of the patriots.

1819   Simón Bolívar's victory in the Battle of Boyacá seals Colombia's independence.

1820   The independence of Ecuador is declared.

1821   Simón Bolívar's victory in the Battle of Carabobo seals the independence of Venezuela.

                Peru's independence is proclaimed on July 22.

1822   The Cry of Ipiranga takes place on September 7. The independence of Brazil from the Portuguese Crown is proclaimed. A monarchic regime is adopted, led by Don Pedro I, who is proclaimed Brazil's emperor on December 12.

                Antonio José de Sucre's victory in the Battle of Pichincha seals the independence of Ecuador.

1824   Antonio José de Sucre and Simón Bolívar's victory in the Battle of Ayacucho seals the independence of Peru.

1828	The book *Elementos de Hijiene* (Elements of Hygiene) by José Félix Melizalde is published in Bogotá, Colombia.
1848	The *Manual del cocinero práctico* (Handbook of the Practical Cook) by Antonia and Isabel Errázuriz is published in Valparaíso, Chile.
1853	The work *Manual de artes, oficios, cocina y repostería* (Handbook of Arts, Trades, Cooking, and Baking) is published in Bogotá, Colombia.
1861	The text entitled *Cocina campestre* (Country Cooking) is published in Venezuela as part of the work *El agricultor venezolano* (The Venezuelan Farmer) by José A. Díaz.
1866	The *Manual de buen gusto que facilita el modo de hacer los dulces, budines, colaciones y pastas y destruye los errores en tantas recetas mal copiadas* (Handbook of Good Taste that Facilitates the Preparation of Sweet Dishes, Puddings, Cookies, and Pastries, and Eliminates the Mistakes Made During the Copying of So Many Recipes), by Valentín Ibáñez, is published in Arequipa, Peru.
1868	The first edition of the work *Colección de medicamentos indígenas* (Collection of Native Medicines), by Gerónimo Pompa, is published in Puerto Cabello, Venezuela.
1889	Brazil is proclaimed a republic on November 15.
1890	Juana Manuela Gorriti's work *Cocina ecléctica* (Eclectic Cuisine) is published in Argentina.
1893	*El cocinero práctico* (The Practical Cook) is published in Quito, Ecuador, under the initials A. G.
1900–2000	In the early twentieth century, the first electrical appliances (gas and kerosene stoves, fridges) start to be imported to South America, mainly from the United States.
1928	First institute for nutritional matters in South America, the Instituto de Nutrición de Argentina, is founded.
1931	Brazil establishes a National Coffee Department. The collapse of the world coffee market brings about an economic disaster and helps precipitate a revolt in the southern provinces. The Coffee Department aims to supervise the destruction of large quantities of Brazil's chief export item in order to maintain good prices in the world market.

1945   Food and Agriculture Organization (FAO) is founded.

1950s   Importation of electric stoves, blenders, and other household
                        appliances such as microwaves begins to increase, while the
                        food industry also begins to expand (canned and frozen foods
                        and pasteurized milk, among others).

1970s–2004   Professional culinary art schools are founded in South America.

1

Historical Overview

The South American continent, which begins with the eastern border of the Republic of Panama, has a total area of more than 7 million square miles, roughly twice as large as the United States. This vast territory represents 12 percent of the earth's surface. It consists of 12 independent countries and a French colony. From north to south, these countries are Venezuela, Colombia, Guyana, Suriname, Ecuador, Brazil, Peru, Bolivia, Chile, Paraguay, Uruguay, and Argentina, plus the French overseas department called French Guiana. The South American population amounts to slightly more than 350 million inhabitants (almost 6 percent of the world's population), 75 percent of whom currently live in cities. Two languages are mainly spoken in this continent: Spanish and Portuguese. However, in some regions people commonly speak indigenous languages, such as Quechua and Aymaran (Peru and Bolivia) or Guarani (Paraguay). Catholicism is the major religion.

Since this sociopolitical scene is the result of a lengthy history, its fundamental cultural and historical milestones are provided for the context needed to understand South American food culture.

THE PEOPLE

Giving a historical account of the current South American societies is not an easy task, because they go back thousands of years and are characterized by considerable complexity and cultural variety. Therefore, the most relevant aspects will be presented, as well as examples that would allow the most comprehensive overview as possible. Many issues related to the history of this continent remain controversial. There are still debates on the origins of the human being in the Americas and, particularly, the first inhabitants of that region. There are some areas, such as the tropical rain forest, that lack a precise historical account, because not enough archaeological excavations have been carried out there. Besides, there are still important gaps concerning the post-Colombian period, especially in terms of regional history.

Indigenous Peoples

According to archaeologists and anthropologists, the vast continental territory called South America was settled by successive waves of immigrants coming from Central America and the Pacific Islands. Most specialists agree that the first settlers of the North American continent arrived from Asia through the Bering Strait during the Pleistocene Era (40,000–35,000 B.C.) and that they continued south along the Pacific coast of North America toward Mexico, Central America, and South America. They were primitive people using roughly carved stone tools. They were nomadic hunter-gatherers, who traveled along the route as they acquired their means of subsistence. Though at a slow pace, this first migration wave eventually reached the southern end of the continent. In the years that followed, approximately 12,000–10,000 B.C., a second wave of settlers entered through the same northern point. They also owned lithic tools, but these were somewhat more developed. This second wave more or less followed the same route to the south.

Other scholars believe another migration wave entered through the southern part of the continent on the side of the Pacific Ocean. These experts argue that there are cultural similarities between Polynesians and South American Indians, including the use of artificial irrigation, the production of chicha (a cold drink made with corn), chieftaincy, the triangular plaited sail, and the sweet potato, among others.

Those people who went to live in South America underwent a cultural evolution, and some of them even carried out agricultural practices. For example, archaeologists have found evidence of both the cultivation of potatoes (Solanum tuberosum) on Peru's Cordillera Oriental and Cordillera Central (eastern and central mountain ranges), which can be traced to around 8000–6000 B.C., and of corn (Zea mays) in Ecuador and Peru to around 3100–1750 B.C. There is also indication of the growing of manioc

(*Manihot esculenta*) in Colombia and Venezuela, dating back to approximately 1500 B.C.

Such agricultural development implied that these people had adopted a sedentary lifestyle. This is how the first villages and cities started to appear in some areas. When one comes to this point in history, it is almost inevitable to think about the Inca Empire, but it is important to make clear that long before this domination took place, a number of other important cultures had existed, which are referred to as the pre-Inca cultures. Some of the most significant are the Chavin culture (1000–200 B.C.), which settled on the northern part of the Andean mountain range (Cordillera Andina) of what is now Peru and is considered to be the oldest Andean culture; the Paracas culture (400–100 B.C.) and the subsequent Nazca culture (0–800 A.D.), which took hold along the southern coast of Peru and the north of Chile; the Mochica civilization (0–600 A.D.) and the Tiahuanaco or Tiwanacu culture (100–1000 A.D.), which settled in what is now Bolivia; the Huari people (600–1100 A.D.), who had an influence on the Peruvian northern, central, and southern mountains; and the Chimu culture (900–1400 A.D.). Other cultures developed in what is now Venezuela and Colombia, namely the Timoto-Cuica and the Chibcha or Muisca cultures, which settled in the *altiplano central* (central high plateau), and the Tayrona culture, which took hold in the mountain range known as Sierra Nevada de Santa Marta. The empire found by Europeans when they arrived on the Pacific coasts of South America (i.e., the Inca Empire) had extended all the way from the border of Colombia and Ecuador (in the north) down to central-northern Chile (in the south). They were a rigorously structured civilization in terms of their political organization. The ruling sovereign was the Inca emperor; just below him was his family and the military, which he used to preserve his power; then followed a great number of officials and farmworkers. They did not have a writing system, but they kept numerical and factual records with an accounting system they had invented of knots on strings of different length and color called *quipus*. Cities and villages surrounded by fields had developed in this vast land, where everything was linked by an extraordinarily built and preserved road system. Two main roads went from north to south—one along the coast and the other one along the mountain—with various intersections at the most important and strategic points. Along these trails there were carefully spaced way stations called *tambos* that served as storehouses and shelters for the messengers and the soldiers, who needed to rest and stock up with provisions. In cities such as Cuzco and Quito, apart from ordinary housing, they had built enormous palaces, temples, and fortresses with stone slabs so finely cut that they fit perfectly when put together. Even today, there are traces of those magnificent buildings in the Peruvian and Bolivian Andes. The emperor was considered a direct descendant of God, so he married his sisters to guarantee pure-blood descendants. By the third decade of the sixteenth century, the Inca emperor had died without having decided which one of his two sons—Huascar or Atahualpa—would be the next emperor, so the two brothers fought each other for control of the empire and in the process placed its unity at risk.

Specialists in historical demography have not agreed yet on the number of inhabitants of the Inca Empire. However, some of them accept the hypothesis that this empire comprised no fewer than 30 million people. It is very difficult to estimate the rest of the pre-Columbian South American population, because it was represented by nomadic tribes and a cluster of villages that have been identified only by means of unsystematic archaeological excavations, and because chroniclers of the conquest period have not provided useful data on the issue.

A great number of tribes emerged in the rest of the continent (in the Venezuelan coast and plains, the Orinoco-Amazonas region and the rest of Brazil) and did not achieve the level of urban development that characterized the Inca. They preserved a nomadic lifestyle or settled in small villages made up of huts or *bohíos*. A very similar panorama characterized Paraguay, Uruguay, and Argentina, where the Guarani and the Charrua people constituted the main ethnic groups. In Chile, the Araucanian people were the most relevant ethnic group, and finally, in the Southern Cone, there were the Patagonians. The wide range of names and locations was a result of the existence of different cultures, among which were different levels of agricultural development and culinary practices. This was more or less the map of the South American ethnic groups before the arrival of the Europeans.

Some of the cuisines of the South American indigenous population will now be described. For simplicity, a general overview will be presented instead of a detailed account of the variety of diets recorded by the very different native cultures in the past. Their diet was based on the use of corn and cassava, supplemented with some leguminous plants as well as animal proteins obtained through hunting and fishing or through the domestication of animals, plus the use of a natural sweetening substance: honey. Their cuisine barely contained fats. Hot pepper was the condiment of choice, although in the Andean region they used certain herbs like *huacatay*, as well as rock salt; in the coastal regions they used sea salt, though always in small quantities. The indigenous people knew how to make the best use of fire. They had learned how to cook their food by placing it directly upon the heat or grilling it on wooden sticks (*barbacoa*) in order to smoke it. They sometimes just placed their food over the embers or on flat pottery made of fired clay (*budares* or *aripos*), or even covered the food with leaves and buried it to cook it over stones that had been previously stacked and heated by a fire until ready to be used as a heat source (*pachamanca*). According to some chroniclers, they built clay containers with their hands, which they used to boil liquids by placing them over three stones of similar size that surrounded their fires, although most of the time boiling was achieved by dropping hot stones inside the pots. In the Andean region they mastered practices to preserve certain foods like *camelidae* meat or game, as well as tubers and fruits that used to be dried by exposure to the sun or to the very low temperatures of the high plateaus called *páramos*. Their cooking utensils included baskets; stone knives and axes; mortars or *metates*; wooden graters and spoon-like spatulas; containers made of certain dried fruits, like the fruit of the *totumo* or calabash tree (*Crescentia cujete*) or the pumpkin (*Cucurbita máxima*); and pottery.

The Indians did not use any tables, because they ate sitting on the ground, putting the containers on leaves. They were not used to talking or drinking water during meals. In the Andean region they ate three times a day, while the tribes of the tropical zone only had two meals.

Their dishes were not as simple as it is commonly believed. Some good examples of this sophistication would be the preparation of the *casabe* and the *cachiri* (from Amazonia), as well as the *arepa*, the *humita* and the *chicha* (from the Andes). The *casabe* is a bread made from bitter cassava (*Manihot esculenta*)—a tuber that contains lethal hydrocyanic acid. Preparing it involves using meticulous techniques, which range from shredding the pulp and squeezing out the poisonous juice (*yare*), to then baking big round flat breads about half a centimeter (1/4 inch) thick from the obtained flour (*catibía*) on round clay griddles.

Such extraordinary culinary techniques should be considered innovations of high value, taking into account that countless humans relied upon the end product for sustenance for at least two millennia. The *casabe* was also the first food the Indians could put into storage, which provided them with a means of survival during shortages.

Corn (*Zea mays*)—another staple food in the indigenous cuisine—was used for the preparation of different dishes. Making *arepas* (another type of native bread) required the application of a number of techniques: first, the grains had to be removed from the corncobs once they had been dried;

then, they had to be boiled and ground in the *metate* until a dough was obtained, which was shaped into small flat balls and then cooked on a *budare* placed over the embers. The *humita* or *huminta* was a bread bun made from fresh corn (*choclo*) wrapped in its leaves and then boiled. As for the *chicha,* its preparation required not only separating the kernels from the corncobs, but also fermenting and grinding the corn, which was often performed by women who chewed it.

It did not take long for this scene to change when the Europeans arrived and extended their dominance, which implied the extermination of a large number of natives by means of simple elimination, the transmission of diseases that did not previously exist in the continent, the pasture of *camelidae* (llama, vicuña, and alpaca), and the changes made to the land farming system and the diet itself.

Europeans

In 1498 Italian navigator Christopher Columbus decided to embark on his third journey, in order to return to the islands he had "discovered" six years earlier. In the beginning of August of that same year, he accidentally landed in the south coast of the island of Trinidad because of a miscalculation, and sailed into the Gulf of Paria near the mouth of the Orinoco River, where he sighted for the first time the north coasts of South America. At first, he thought he had landed in the coast of a huge island. It was not until some time later that he realized he had reached a continent. This geographical fact was confirmed with the subsequent voyages of Columbus and other sailors serving the king and queen of Spain. This region comprising the east, north, and west coasts of Venezuela was called Tierra Firme (mainland). Following in Columbus's footsteps, the Florentine navigator Amerigo Vespucci also decided to travel to the new continent, although he claimed he had reached its coasts before Columbus, in 1497. This man is particularly interesting because the New World Columbus had discovered was named after Vespucci. How is this possible? In 1507, in a small town of Lorraine called Saint Die, a group of scholarly men decided to revise Ptolemy's well-known *Geography*, and since they had read Vespucci's letter regarding his journey and his claim of having found a New World, they decided to include it at the end of the treatise, which was published in 1507 under the title *Cosmographiae Introductio*. It stated that a new continent had been discovered and they decided to designate it America in honor of the Florentine seafarer. They also included in this work a world map made by one of the editors, Martin Waldseemüller, in which the word "America" was used to name the recently discovered lands that corresponded to South America. But it was not until 1538, when the famous cartographer Mercator published his well-known *Atlas*, that this name started to be applied also to the north portion of the New World. Since then, there was not only a South America, but also a North America. The work published in 1507 was so successful that in that same year seven editions had been produced, which enabled the quick spreading of the name America.

The remarkable discoveries carried out at the end of the fifteenth century and thereafter were due to the actions taken by the kingdoms of Spain and Portugal—the only European nations that were relevant naval powers at that time. They were known for the large number of extraordinarily courageous and vigorous domestic and foreign sailors, explorers, and soldiers who had decided to serve these nations, winning for them most of the discovered lands. Soon after the explorations began, a great rivalry broke out between the Spanish and the Portuguese regarding the rights they had or would have in the future over the New World. As was usual at that time, the two rivals decided that their controversy on the possible rights to conquer and colonize those lands would be settled by the then pope, Alexander VI. In May 1493, the pope issued a bull called *Inter caetera*, which drew an imaginary line on the globe 100 leagues west of the Azores islands and granted the Spanish all lands to the west of the line and the Portuguese those on the east. This line was later moved 270 leagues further west with the Treaty of Tordesillas, signed in June 1494 by the monarchs of the two rival countries. The division decreed by this agreement extended 48 degrees west of the Greenwich Meridian. Taking into consideration that people did not know what the geography of the South American continent was like at that time, it is particularly remarkable that this dividing line coincided almost precisely with a series of well-defined natural obstacles that extended from north to south. The most important of these obstacles was the vast Amazonian rain forest, which buffered against a collision between the two European powers for many years.

So the Spanish and the Portuguese started to conquer territories and establish colonies within the limits that had been set for them. This was an easier enterprise for the Spanish, because they found well-organized government systems dependent on a central power, like in the case of Nueva Granada (now Colombia) and Peru, which enabled them—by taking control over the supreme centers of power—to dominate the rest of the population, which was accustomed to submitting to authority without resistance. Before the end of the sixteenth century, the Spanish colonial empire had reached its peak in terms of geographic expansion. Between 1520 and 1590 no fewer than 60 cities were founded, among which are the capitals of the Spanish-speaking countries that exist today, except for Montevideo, which was founded in 1726. These capital cities were Quito (1534), Lima (1535), Buenos Aires (1536), Asunción (1537), Bogotá (1538), Santiago de Chile (1541), La Paz (1548), and Caracas (1567).

Around 25,000 Spaniards are estimated to have traveled from Spain to South America from 1493 to 1600. However, the white population residing in this portion of the New World is said to have amounted to 85,500 inhabitants by the year 1570, while the African slaves, mestizos (a mix of indigenous and white), and mulattoes (a mix of black and white) numbered 169,000. The estimated number of the indigenous population was some 5,750,000. This demographic description reveals the growing number of Spanish descendants, as well as a significant increase in the number of descendants resulting from the mix of Spanish and the rest of the population. It also shows that there was still a very large number of indigenous people.

The Portuguese are said to have proceeded at a slower pace, as they had to deal with rebel tribes located in what is now Brazil and spread throughout large expanses of land. They settled along the Atlantic coasts and were left exposed to attacks from indigenous tribes from the interior or from other European sailing nations coming from the sea, as was the case of the French and the Dutch. During the same period used to account for the number of cities founded by the Spanish, the Portuguese only managed to establish 11 new cities. Three of them are still very important nowadays: Pernambuco (1536), Bahia (1549), and Rio de Janeiro (1565). They would have probably been more successful if they had not embarked on the project of establishing and maintaining an empire in the East Indies at the same time. Besides, Portugal's population and resources were much smaller than those of the Spanish.

The contingent of conquerors and colonizers was heterogeneous. As for Spain, there were Andalusians, Castilians, Catalans, Basques, Aragonese, and Galicians. It can be said that the notion of the "Spanish people" emerged in the Americas, because the different Iberian countries that embarked on the venture of colonizing it had to remain together in the new lands as a whole block in order to be able to confront the indigenous people. Especially during the first years, those who set sail for the new continent were men who left their families in Europe or who were single.

This was a military undertaking. They had to fight their inhabitants to win new lands and subjugate them. So the number of European women who went to South America was not significant. This factor contributed to the mixing that took place between the Spanish and the indigenous people.

Giving a general account of the European conquerors' diet is as challenging as describing that of the natives. In fact, this task would even result in a more significant distortion of reality, because by the fifteenth century the Iberian Peninsula—only referring to the Spanish and the Portuguese—featured very precise and well-differentiated gastronomic regions. These regions were so different that it is very difficult to generalize in order to present a diet that applies to all the Iberian societies. Geographers have developed a gastronomic regionalization that could be used to give an account of the European diet, although it dates from the twentieth century. It records food traditions and habits that could perfectly apply to the time before the discovery of the Americas if some adjustments are made. In this sense, a main difference has been set between the Mediterranean and the so-called Central European diets. The Mediterranean diets include those of the former kingdoms of Andalusia, Granada, Murcia, Valencia, Aragon, Catalonia, New Castile, a fair portion of Old Castile, Leon, Galicia, Asturias, the Basque Country, Navarre, and a large strip of land on the north of Aragon along the Pyrenees, as well as central and southern Portugal. The basic difference between these two diets is the use of lipoids: the Mediterranean cuisine is characterized by the use of vegetable fat, specifically olive oil, while the Central European one is known for that of animal fat, specifically lard or butter. Actually, the Mediterranean diet is basically vegetarian, whereas the Central European diet is meat-based.

A number of other differences in these two cuisines could be certainly mentioned here, but the common gastronomic features represent a diet similar to that of the Iberian conquerors who came to the New World. The most important common features are the use of wheat and wine. Wheat is Europe's grain of choice when it comes to making any type of bread. All Iberian regions use it, although barley, rye, and oats were also commonly used with that purpose, but to a lesser extent. In any case, wheat has played the most important role, because since the beginnings of Christianity it has been associated with religion, as bread made of wheat was the only one that could be used for transubstantiation (i.e., consecrated in the Mass and considered to be the body of the risen Jesus). Grapes are another key component of the European food culture. Wine was incorporated into religion too, as it was declared holy to represent the blood of Christ in the Eucharistic sacrament, again by means of its transubstantiation.

Apart from these two basic elements, some others that also featured in the conquerors' typical diet, though to a lesser extent, are European tubers (mainly turnips and carrots), bulbs (garlic, onions, chives, shallots, leeks), stalks (celery, borage), leafy vegetables (cabbage, chard, spinach, lettuce, endive, thistle), other garden vegetables (eggplant, cucumber, red cabbage, squash), products from the orchard (citrus, figs, pomegranates, almond fruit, peaches, quinces, olives), legumes (chickpeas, broad beans), rice, and a great variety of aromatic plants (oregano, coriander, parsley, thyme, marjoram, rosemary, bay, mint) and others that were used as condiments (saffron, capers). As for the meat, there were (in order of importance) pork, beef, sheep, goat, poultry, and some game such as partridge, wild boar, and venison. It is also essential to mention a great variety of fish and shellfish caught in the Mediterranean Sea, the Atlantic Ocean, and the different freshwaters.

Salt and honey were very ubiquitous in Iberian dishes. Later, they also started using cane sugar, as a result of the Arab influence. In the book *Libro de agricultura*, written by Abu Zacaría in the twelfth century, there are already records of sugar production. The use of some spices from the Far East—such as pepper, cloves, nutmeg, and cinnamon—also spread throughout the peninsula.

The Iberian cooking utensils were mainly made of metal or fired clay. The cutlery was made of iron, as were gridirons, frying pans, cauldrons, skewers, mortars, ladles, spoons, skimmers, and carving knives and forks. Some saucepans were made of copper. Pitchers, deep pans, plates, trays, and so on were made of china. Bottles, glasses, and different types of bowls were made of glass. Some silver pieces should be also mentioned, as well as mortars that were made of stone or wood.

Iberians cooked on stoves using different methods: stewing, frying, baking, or roasting.

The peninsular food culture was first influenced by the Goths, the Greeks, and the Romans in ancient times. Then the Arabs came and certainly left their mark as a result of their long domination in a significant portion of the territory.

The Iberian culinary practices had been recorded since the early Middle Ages in cookbooks that had been written by hand in royal courts and convents. The books written in the convents are especially significant, because many of the religious orders that established houses and convents in the South American continent brought with them their food culture.

Africans

Throughout history all conquests have been characterized by the presence of violence, and that of the Americas was no exception. The indigenous people not only submitted to the authority of the Europeans, but to a greater extent they were also enslaved by them. The natives were forced into hard labor, which resulted in a considerable decrease in their population. Although the Spanish monarchs decreed laws to protect the natives, many atrocities were committed because of the failure to adhere to those laws. Especially in the warm regions, the decrease in the indigenous population—and the subsequent lack of labor force to work in agriculture and mining—gave rise to the trade of African slaves, who were brought to the continent to supplement such deficiency or simply because they were considered to be more resistant to arduous labor and the inclemency of the weather. Africans were brought everywhere throughout the Spanish and Portuguese empires. However, the largest contingents were brought to the equatorial region. This new demographic element, which was culturally heterogeneous, was another ingredient for the mixing that in the end resulted in an extremely diverse population in terms of features and color.

The blacks who were brought to South America were native to the lands stretching from below Cape Verde down to the Cape of Good Hope, bounded by the vast Atlantic coast to the west. It remains unknown exactly how far into the interior of Africa the Europeans penetrated in order to get slaves. The largest contingents of black slaves who were brought to the ports to be sold had probably been found in Africa's interior. The major source area was generically called Guinea. Nevertheless, some of the slaves brought to Brazil—where the slave trade carried on until the middle of the nineteenth century—are said to have been exported from Mozambique and even from some other African locations. A number of scholars who have researched the slave trade from Africa to the American continent have made partial estimates regarding the number of Africans who were brought to South America from the beginning of the conquest to the middle of the nineteenth century. The number of slaves transported to Brazil, for example, has been estimated at 4 million, whereas those delivered in the former Spanish Empire (now the South American Spanish-speaking countries) are said to have amounted to 2.5 million. Although the estimates on these issues remain hypothetical, almost all historians agree that the number of slaves carried from Africa to South America was much larger than that of the Europeans who crossed the Atlantic with that same destination. However, not all South American colonies belonging to the Spanish Empire experienced the same influx of African slaves. For example, Venezuela and Colombia faced the arrival of a greater number of Africans than those brought to Peru and Chile. Before slave trade took place in Africa, the continent featured the coexistence of many cultures with their own typical diets. Although it cannot be said that they were similar in every respect, they can all be integrated for the purpose of this book, presenting a general picture of the African food habits based on the many common characteristics they showed. For example, vegetables played a key role in all African diets. Meat was not a significant food for most of them, as it was often eaten by rich tribe chiefs, the nobility, and a few hunting tribes. The great majority of Africans did not eat it—only very little and on formal occasions. Some tribes, such as the Jolofo and the Mandingo, raised cattle, sheep, and goats. Sheep and goat were eaten more frequently, as their meat was thought to be superior to that of cattle. This was probably due to the fact that cattle used to be attacked by the tsetse fly. The animals that were mostly hunted by the African tribes were the antelope, the oryx, the gazelle, and the hare. There were also certain groups who basically hunted giraffes, hippopotamuses, and elephants. They fished to such an extent, both in the sea and in freshwaters, that fish must be included in this general account of the African food culture.

The diet of the people living in most parts of these areas depended on agriculture, which they practiced through techniques as rudimentary as those used by the Indians in South America. The African diet featured the following key ingredients: three native grains, namely millet (*Pennisetum typhoideum*), sorghum (*Sorghum vulgare*), and a wild rice variety (*Oriza glaberrima*); a rhizome, namely yams (*Dioscorea alata*); a number of legumes, namely cowpeas (*Vigna sinensis*), broad beans (*Vicia faba*), chickpeas (*Cicer arietinum*), and lentils (*Lens culinaris*); as well as squashes, eggplants, cabbages, cucumbers, onions, and garlic. Their typical fruits were melons, watermelons, tamarinds, dates, figs, baobab fruits (*Adansonia digitata*), pomegranates, lemons, and oranges. As sweetening substances they used honey and, to a lesser extent, cane sugar, whose cultivation was introduced in earlier times (the eleventh century) by the Arabs and then (in the fifteenth century) expanded by the Portuguese. Africans used very little salt and seasoned their food with a variety of pepper (*Piper guineense*) and ginger. They also used palm oil (from *Elaeis guineensis*) and a margarine from a tree called *karite* (*Elaeis guineensis*), although sesame oil also played a role to a lesser extent.

Africans used very few utensils to prepare their foods. They used grinding stones, big pounding mortars, dried pumpkins used as bowls, wooden containers and spoons, iron-made knives, and the skin of goats sewed into bags to store grain. They were accustomed to sitting on the ground to eat. They would put their food inside containers generally made of vegetables and place them on leaves they put on the ground.

The stories told by travelers and slave traders, along with the conceptions the Europeans had of the blacks well from the start—that they were strong and had robust constitutions—are why they considered them fit to do the hardest labor, and are what could be a reason to believe that the African diet was highly nutritional.

Other Immigrations

At the beginning of the nineteenth century, a series of pro-independence movements started to emerge, which later on consolidated and put an end to the Spanish domination in the 1820s. Those were the years of the so-called Wars of Independence, which not only caused much shedding of blood in the battlefields and the collapse of the Spanish administration, but also inner migrations, like that of Venezuelans traveling to the south (until they arrived to Peru, Bolivia, or Chile) under the leadership of Simón Bolívar. As is the case in any migration process, people do not travel alone; they carry their customs with them and learn new habits. Without a doubt, this situation laid the foundations for people to get to know each other's traditions, especially food habits. It is very common, therefore, to find Venezuelan recipes in Peruvian traditional cookbooks or Peruvian delicacies within the Venezuelan cuisine. This is the case of *bienmesabe* (a dessert prepared with eggs, sugar, and coconut) or *chupe* (a soup similar to the North American chowders).

Brazil was an exception, because it did not gain its independence by means of a war, but merely through political arrangements. When Napoléon's troops invaded the Iberian Peninsula, threatening the Braganza monarchy of Portugal, King João VI fled with the whole royal family to Brazil, where he ruled until 1821, when he could return to Lisbon, as Portugal had been recovered. He left his son Pedro as regent in his vast New World dominion. In the following year, the latter decided to declare Brazil to be independent of Portugal and was proclaimed constitutional emperor of the new country.

Once they had consolidated the political and social process of their independence from the Iberian Peninsula, the South American countries
strove to establish new trade relationships with Europe, trying to enter
the international economic system. It is important to make a distinc-
tion between the experience of Brazil and that of the remaining territory
that belonged to the Spanish Empire, because the former did not fight
a bloody battle to gain independence, as was the case of the Spanish-
speaking countries. When Brazil became an independent empire ruled
by a descendant of the Braganza family, the immigration policy carried
out in this new country was aimed at encouraging European immigrants
to go to Brazil. In the case of the colonies that had belonged to Spain,
the War of Independence took a long period of time—a bit more than
a decade—during which the immigration policy came to a halt and the
native population decreased because of the enormous loss of life caused
by the conflict. Once this last war had been overcome and the adminis-
trative issues had more or less returned to normal, European immigration
was fostered, playing a more significant role since the 1830s, which is
precisely the moment when the first immigration wave began. Based on
the argument that "peopling means ruling," the South American countries stimulated the import of technology and foreign human capital that
was able to operate it without having to train the local population, which
would have been a slow and expensive process. More than 70 percent
of the 59 million Europeans who left their continent with overseas des-
tinations between 1824 and 1924 went to North America, whereas 21
percent chose Latin America. Half of these 11 million people decided to
go to Argentina, a third chose Brazil as their destination, and a twentieth
went to the small country of Uruguay.

A first migration wave (1835–57) quietly manifested in South America
within the framework of governmental policies aimed at the establishment of farming and craft-based colonies, most of which did not succeed
as expected, resulting in a fall in the population. This first European migration wave mainly headed for the United States. The colonies of Europeans that had settled in South America during the first migration flood
especially included Swiss, German, French, Irish, Welsh, Spanish, and
Italian people, who totaled several tens of thousands of immigrants. Brazil
received the largest number of them, followed by Uruguay, Argentina,
Chile, Peru, and Venezuela.

The second migration wave lasted until 1930 and was more significant
than the first one. The farming population of less industrialized European countries massively migrated to the South American continent, as

well as some Asian contingents from China, India, Syria, and Lebanon, who arrived both in the north and the south of South America. The Japanese mainly went to Brazil. Within this period, there was a better situation in the South American countries, which helped them host a large number of immigrants. In 1880 Europe started to suffer a strong demographic pressure that could not be offset by the less industrialized countries of the Mediterranean or Eastern Europe. As a result, an even larger contingent of people started to migrate to the new continent—a trend that lasted until 1935. Within the framework of this transoceanic immigration movement, Argentina was the leading country in terms of the number of immigrants received, which amounted to 3.4 million between 1881 and 1935. Then followed Brazil, which received 3.3 million immigrants between 1872 and 1940. Most of these people were Italian (the largest contingent), Spanish, Portuguese, French, and—though in smaller amounts—Russian, Turkish, Yugoslavian, Polish, German, English, and Japanese, among other nationalities. In Argentina, at least three-fourths of the total number of immigrants decided to settle permanently.

A third migration movement was triggered by the Spanish Civil War and World War II. In those countries that received the most immigrants, such as Brazil and Argentina, the migration of foreigners into their countries was restricted. Out of the 7,092,000 European emigrants who traveled overseas between 1946 and 1957, 1,757,400 arrived in South America. However, the region soon reopened as an immigration destination, first to Spanish citizens, who headed for Chile and Venezuela during and after the Spanish Civil War, and then to other European citizens fleeing their countries in the postwar period, who chose the most attractive places of the continent from 1946 to 1960, namely Argentina, Brazil, and Venezuela.

The Asian immigrants started to arrive in South America in the mid-nineteenth century. An example would be the Chinese, who were hosted by Peru starting in 1849. Between 1859 and 1874, 87,000 Chinese entered the country, most of them becoming part of the agricultural labor force. By 1876, Asians represented 1.9 percent of the total population of Peru, according to the census carried out that year.

The *turcos*—who were not Turks, incidentally, but mainly Syrian and Lebanese that were so called because of their Middle Eastern origin—started to arrive to South America in 1870. They specialized in retail and peddling, which is the reason why they would have to endure some hostility thereafter. Nevertheless, they showed a great capacity to adapt to the new environment, to some extent due to their physical appearance, which was very similar to that of the Southern Europeans.

While in Argentina most immigrants were European, Brazil recorded a very significant immigration flow of Japanese starting in 1908. Their contribution in terms of the number of immigrants began to grow in a slow but progressive manner, until they became the leading immigrant group and the foreign population that had mostly (92 percent) decided to permanently settle in that country. Japanese immigrants, along with European ones, settled on family farms located in São Paulo State. This contributed considerably to the intensification and diversification of agricultural practices in that region—coffee being the most important agricultural product.

At that time, a great number of workers called "coolies" started to arrive from India. Some of them had been tricked into traveling to South America. In most cases, they escaped from the sugarcane or coffee harvest, or from the laying of railroad tracks to go to the cities, thereby becoming a floating population group that specialized in trade and street peddling and contributed their food habits to some South American countries.

These immigration movements influenced the food culture of the continent by reinforcing the European culinary habits (i.e., their use of wheat and wine, along with their meat-based diet). They did not have the same influence everywhere. It depended on the number of immigrants who arrived to each place, who mostly ended up settling in the cities. While the Asian immigrants—especially Chinese and Japanese—influenced Peru's and Brazil's food cultures, the Guianas and eastern Venezuela were more influenced by the food habits brought from India, out of which the most remarkable contribution is perhaps the use of curry, which remained unknown in the rest of the continent for a long time. It is also important to mention the contribution made by those coming from the Middle Eastern Arab countries, as they helped—along with some Sephardic Jewish immigrants—to spread the enjoyment of some of their typical dishes, such as unleavened bread, the sweets prepared with honey and almonds, and lamb.

The establishment of restaurants was basically carried out by Italians and Spaniards, who wanted to make their typical dishes known. Since 1950, the Chinese also made incursions into the meal-service business, in which they proved to be very successful, so much so that it can be said that it is almost impossible to find a South American village or city without a Chinese restaurant. The type of Chinese food that prevailed in most South American countries was Cantonese. Some of the dishes became very well known, such as spring rolls; rice or noodles with pork, beef, or chicken and vegetables (seasoned with soy sauce); and desserts such as small Chinese oranges and lychees.

Five Centuries of Mixing

During the 500 years that followed Columbus's arrival, a biological as well as cultural mixing took place. The combination of the various food cultures had a different evolution and intensity depending on the time period—whether it was the colonial or the republican times—and the immigration movement taking place. The process was much more intense during the colonial times than afterward, but nowadays South Americans are still suffering changes in their food habits, which are not so much a consequence of the immigration of people anymore, but of the spreading of food habits that are related to the "American way of life" that gains ground thanks to the technological developments in the communication networks and to the penetration of transnational food corporations.

Colonial Times

The mixing process was more intense in colonial times. An expert in the field of the conquest and its cultural effects in Latin America stated the following:

In the field of folk culture, in a somewhat limited sense of the term, the processes at work in the acceptance or rejection of the Spanish elements by Indian cultures are less clear than in the two foregoing categories. We are dealing here with areas of culture not of primary concern to State and Church and with areas of culture in which obvious superiority either does not exist or cannot be easily recognized. This is an area in which chance, and perhaps the personality of unusual individuals, both Spanish and Indian, seems to have played an unusual role. With respect to such things as dietary patterns, superstitions, folk medicine, folklore, and music, Spanish traits found themselves in competition with indigenous traits, and often with no clear advantage.[1]

At first, the conquerors depended on the indigenous population to get their food, so they got used to eating corn, cassava, and potatoes, as well as tropical fruits such as pineapple, guava and soursop, among others. However, they never abandoned the hopes they had of reproducing their food culture in the new lands, so as soon as they managed to pacify a territory and establish cities, they started to transfer the vegetables and animals of Europe to the new continent. An example of what Europeans brought to

South America within this agricultural colonization process would be the harvest of sugar cane and the processing techniques to obtain sugar from it. This product faced fierce rejection by the indigenous people. Some chroniclers of that time recorded that this sweetening substance would not only make them feel sick, but also cause stomach problems, so they considered it to be a cause for illness. Indians had a very similar reaction toward meat, be it pork, beef, or sheep.

The Spanish were used to eating a lot and at least three times a day, mainly because they had suffered real hardship in their homeland in the past. So they tried to impose their dietary patterns on the indigenous population from the start, but these people had always been moderate in their eating habits and suffered greatly. Some of them even died because of the health-related problems arising from this imposition. Father Joseph de Acosta, in his book entitled *Historia natural y moral de las Indias* (Natural and Moral History of the Indies), wrote that one of the key causes for the fall of the indigenous population may have been this change in their diet imposed by the conquerors.[2] Nevertheless, it seems that the conquerors never considered this to be a cause for an increase in mortality, as they held that the products and food habits they were used to in Europe were superior to those of the indigenous people. Their way of thinking is illustrated in the following quotation from a defender of the Spanish colonization, the Jesuit José Nuix y Perpiñá, in 1780:

The arts and the industry were brought to those people by the Spanish. They immediately provided them with the tools needed to work the land and to manufacture the most utilitarian goods. The deserts were filled with the animals needed for agricultural, culinary and other practices. New fruits suddenly appeared on the landscape, while the fields fulfilled the expectations and desires of the new growers. The forests had been abandoned; the laborious hunting and hazardous fishing practices were no longer carried out. The Natives did not live in their huts anymore, but in comfortable and healthy dwelling places. *They started to eat more nutritious, delicious and ordinary food* [italics added]; they stopped being naked and, at the end, they were ashamed of their previous condition.[3]

This opinion is certainly typical of the conquerors' way of thinking and does not exactly correspond to what really happened. Especially in the countries with predominantly indigenous population (Colombia, Ecuador, Peru, and Bolivia), most of the natives maintained their pre-Hispanic food habits for centuries. It is true, though, that a food hierarchy was established, according to which the European edible plants (wheat, grapevines, and olives) were considered to be superior to those of the New World (corn, cassava, and beans).

However, there is no doubt that after all this rejection, the Indians adopted some of the European foods, while the Europeans definitely accepted many of the native ones as part of their culinary repertoire. For example, in the beginning of the conquest, Europeans replaced quince (*Cydonia vulgaris* Pers) with guava (*Psidium guajava* Raddy) to be able to prepare the typical Spanish jam. They also began to use annatto (*Bixa orellana* L.) because of the lack of saffron (*Carthamus tinctorius* L.), which was very much used by the Spanish to dye their foods.

During the eighteenth century new tree species were brought to South America. One of them, and probably the most important one, is the mango (*Manguifera indica* L.), which acclimatized so quickly and spread so effectively throughout the whole equatorial region of the continent that many people thought it was native to the New World—although it had originated in India, as its name suggests. Another tree that was brought to the continent—in this case from the Pacific Islands—was the breadfruit tree (*Artocarpus communis* Forst.), which is usually associated to the famous *Bounty* ship sent to transplant it; the nutmeg (*Myristica fragrans* L.) and the tamarind (*Tamarindus indica* L.) were also some of these "transoceanic plants."

By the eighteenth century, the cultural-mixing process that has been referred to had brought about a type of cuisine that was practiced by the members of the South American societies called *criollas*, as they in turn resulted from the mixing of the various ethnic groups. There is a phrase that has been found in documents dating from that century that helps to define what this type of cuisine is about, namely "eating the country's own way."

Republican Times

During the nineteenth and the early twentieth century, as already mentioned, South America received new waves of immigration, which allowed for the arrival of some other new foods. The influx of Europeans at that time, for example, gave a boost to import trade, allowing for the entrance of beer, turkeys raised in North America, and some tree species like those of mandarin, grapefruit, and macadamia. New animals also arrived in South America during this period, including fish such as trout and salmon. These were mainly bred in the Andean region, from Venezuela and Colombia (trout) down to Chile and Argentina (trout and salmon). Other important transplants were those of soy, sorghum, and fruits such as kiwis and raspberries.

But perhaps the most important innovation that took place in South America during the twentieth century regarding food habits was the emergence of fast food, as a result of the basically urban trend toward the adoption of the "American way of life." The first food that emerged within this context in South America was the hot dog, which came to be so successful—always in the urban environment—that by 1930 one could already buy hot dogs in food stands on the street. The hamburger would come next and rapidly spread throughout the region. Compared to the hot dog, it was preferred in later times, because it was promoted by large multinational corporations. Today, fast food restaurants selling hamburgers in any South American city within everyone's price range has without doubt resulted in its remarkable popularization.

It is also remarkable that there have been some interesting cases of indigenous fast foods. In Venezuela, the *arepas* (type of breads made with corn) have been the most popular food for as long as memory can recall. They started to be sold in the 1950s in small restaurants called *areperas*, where one could have them with either cheese, shredded or stewed meat, black beans, or many other fillings, plus a *batido* (fruit shake). This snack, which one could have very quickly and even standing, was equivalent to a complete meal. These types of small restaurants can compete with and sometimes even overshadow those selling foreign fast food.

EVOLUTION OF AGRICULTURE AND STOCK BREEDING

The inhabitants of South America, like those of the other continents, have gone through all the different evolutionary stages throughout history concerning their relationship with the environment. Such stages have not excluded each other, but have rather overlapped during the transition phases. As a result, different ways of life coexist nowadays, ranging from gatherer tribes to contemporary agro-industrial enterprises. In between these two extremes, intermediate agricultural and stock-breeding practices are found in the region even today. So anyone who would travel throughout the whole South American region to conduct research on the issue would certainly be in touch with all the different traces that make up the history of agriculture. Some manifestations of the most representative milestones in the evolution of food procurement will be presented here in chronological order, with a brief description of some of them, as well as remarks on their technological evolution since then and how the various ways of life have survived until the present.

The first example to be introduced is that of the foraging peoples, whose description has triggered much discussion among anthropologists.

The pre-Columbian agricultural practices, especially the small production units called *conucos* (in Venezuela and Colombia), *chacras* (in Ecuador, Peru, and Chile), or *roças* (in Brazil), will be particularly referred to. Then, terrace cultivation, known as *andenes* in the whole South American Andean region, will be mentioned. There will of course be allusions to the production units that appeared with the arrival of the Europeans, that is, the haciendas (plantations) that allowed for the flourishing of the colonial agriculture characterized by the production of many commercial fruits, such as cacao and coffee. This evolution culminates in the creation of plantations devoted to agro-industry. Finally, the domesticated animals will be discussed, both those native to the New World and those brought by the Europeans to be part of their farms and stockyards.

Gathering, Hunting, and Fishing

The early studies in ethnology considered the so-called primitive peoples to be essentially nomadic and gatherers. Later, they were also referred to as hunters and fishermen. These categories have been used for a long time to describe them, but modern anthropologists have concluded that it is very unlikely that those peoples had simply been gatherers or solely gatherers, hunters, and fishermen, as research on such ways of life has shown that the primitive peoples developed the domestication of plants to a certain extent due to their foraging needs. So if one of these groups specialized in the gathering of a certain type of fruit, it would then gain knowledge—through practice and observation—on the growth of the plants that produced that specific type of fruit, as well as on the appropriate time of year to harvest them. These people would even start to introduce changes to the plants, paving the way for their domestication. A similar process took place regarding their habits and the distribution of animals throughout the lands. This basic relationship with nature that was aimed at searching for ways to meet their needs for food provision, clothing, and housing led to the development of agricultural and stock-breeding practices that would result in the establishment of the group in a fixed place and, therefore, in its transition to civilization.

The nomadic peoples living principally from gathering, hunting, and fishing inhabited the vast rain forest area lying in the basins of the Orinoco and the Amazon rivers. Some examples are the ethnic groups from the linguistic families Tupi-Guarani and Arawak, who were established in the areas between the two rivers. But those peoples who resided on the lands near the rivers—which were prone to flooding—developed simple agricultural practices thanks to natural irrigation in a relatively short time. Some of these primitive tribes are still found in Venezuela, Brazil, Colombia, Ecuador, and Peru. They have preserved their pre-Columbian Neolithic lifestyle with very little change. An example of the current times would be the Nukak peoples, who are part of the Maku group along with other hunter-gatherer tribes of the northwestern part of the Amazon basin. These people first came into contact with missionaries in the 1980s. Even though they incorporated the use of metal utensils like pots and machetes, they continued living according to their old customs in general terms. Their staple food is cassava, which they now combine with other manufactured products such as threshed rice, refined sugar, and pasta they buy in town stores. They are still hunters, and their favorite game includes monkey, *báquiro* (peccary), terrapin, *lapa* (paca) or agouti, and certain birds. They have significant knowledge of plants, and it can be said that they are on the way to becoming farmers.

Simple Agricultural Practices

The infant agriculture practiced by South Americans before the arrival of Columbus was based on the slash-and-burn farming method, which involves clearing a patch of forest by cutting the trees and shrubs and setting them on fire, in order to make the land fit to grow the crops. Even though the nutrient-rich ashes served as natural fertilizers, the soil was depleted in a relatively short time period, so they had to clear a new land patch and shift their cultivation. This traveling form of agriculture was in keeping with the nomadic lifestyle of primitive farmers.

The agricultural tools used were almost entirely limited to the *macana* (a solid wooden sword-like weapon with fire-hardened sharp edges) and stone axes used to cut down the trees, as well as the digging stick. The latter was used to dig holes where cuttings (as for cassava), root sprouts (potatoes), or seeds (corn) would be inserted. They did not know of the plow, nor did they scatter seeds. Their small sown fields or *conucos* are still found in some regions of South America. They have been used to harvest crops in almost the same way for as long as memory can recall, although in republican and more recent times they started to be fought as they were considered a bad agricultural practice. Traditionally, the crops grown in *conucos* were cassava or corn, beans, and pumpkins, and later also fruit trees, both native (guava, soursop, etc.) and foreign (citrus and banana).

Developing Agriculture

The development of the South American agriculture mainly took place in the Andean region by the sedentary peoples that established clusters of villages, like the Timoto-Cuica (Venezuela), important kingdoms like the Chibcha (Colombia), and, last but not least, the Inca Empire or Tawuantinsuyo (Peru, Ecuador, and Bolivia). The agricultural practices recorded in the Andean region included irrigation; fertilization, with *guano* (bird droppings) in Peru, or manure from llamas, vicuñas, and alpacas; terracing (necessary in those mountainous lands); and seed (corn) and tuber (potato) selection. The terraces built on the mountain slopes were particularly significant; they were called *andenes* because they were typical of the Andean mountain range. This system involved the creation of various levels at different heights, where they could experiment on the cultivation of different species. This allowed them to find out which was the best habitat for the cultivation of certain seeds, as was the case of the various corn and potato varieties. The Andean peoples did not have plows either, so they also used the digging stick to break up the land, as did their fellow peoples from the tropical rain forest.

The Inca Empire not only recorded significant agricultural practices, but also a very effective system of storage and distribution of crops, along with an organized farming regime that allowed for an alternation of the harvest of the emperor's lands with that of communal and even private holdings.

Commercial Agriculture

The arrival of the conquerors brought about the establishment of production units that were larger than the *conucos* and generally devoted to only one kind of crop, while the *andenes* were abandoned to a great extent. These new units were the haciendas, which were mainly used to grow fruits destined for exportation. They were also intended for the cultivation of highly demanded cultures that would be sold in the domestic market. Europeans brought the plow, which was only used on flat or less rough terrains. This was an unknown tool in the New World, and the type brought by the Europeans to their colonies was the one used in Andalusia (Spain). Plows were pulled by oxen yoked by the horns and mainly used in the sugar-cane plantations—a plant native to Asia that had been brought by the Arabs to Spain through the African northern coast, and then transferred to the Americas.

The other important fruits cultivated in the haciendas were cacao (native to South America, according to the latest paleobotanical studies) and coffee (native to Asia, and introduced in the eighteenth century in the Caribbean region and then in Brazil and the rest of the continent). Due to their intrinsic characteristics, the cultivation of these two cultures did not allow for much mechanization, except for the processing phase. The harvest had to be performed manually, as did the weeding and the plantations' maintenance.

The haciendas had been established by the conquerors and their descendants, and since the agricultural practices carried out in them were of an extensive nature, their owners were always keen to extend their holdings however possible. This is how large estates came into existence. Within the vast haciendas there continued to be *conucos*, small *chacras*, or *roças*, as the farmworkers and even slaves were allowed to have their own sown fields, both for their subsistence and in order to provide the neighboring haciendas and villages with food products that were called "the fruits of the country." The evolution of the haciendas not only resulted in the appropriation of vast expanses of land, but also in the establishment of facilities to process the fruits: *trapiches* or *ingenios* (i.e., sugar-cane mills), and *oficinas* or *talleres* (for cacao and coffee processing). It was in these places that mechanization took place, at first depending on the force of the humans or beasts (oxen, mules, and donkeys), then on steam, and finally on electric power.

The haciendas were real power and population centers. Especially in Brazil, cities originated mainly as a result of the plantations established both by colonists and missionaries.

The Agro-Industry

In the middle of the twentieth century, modern production units started to be founded, featuring a much higher degree of mechanization and an economic organization aimed at producing fruits on a large scale to be processed in the newly established food industries. A great technological transfer had taken place, which was aimed, in the food sector, at the production of canned and packed foods—flours and other precooked products—to meet the demands of the growing urban population. This form of agricultural production began to gradually overshadow the role of the haciendas, and it is currently the most important food-production source. At this stage of the process, a great number of foreign corporations with highly developed know-how arrived in the Americas. The large agro-industrial companies started to compete with the *hacendados* (landowners) and, obviously, with the still surviving *conuqueros* (smallholders) too. Canned foods were already used when these large foreign enterprises were established; since the end of the nineteenth century, consumption of canned foods had become a habit because of the growing importation of these types of products. Large sugar and corn mills, along with factories of sardine and other canned fish, are some good examples of this new stage that transformed the plantation world that had prevailed for a couple of centuries.

In any case, none of the breakthroughs in the field of agriculture that have been briefly presented here completely replaced the previously existing forms of land use, which is why old and modern agricultural practices coexist today.

Domesticated Animals in Pre-Columbian Times

When the Europeans first arrived in South America, they thought the domestication of animals had not yet taken place. Very soon, though, as they conquered that part of the New World, they realized that the domestication of animals and even stock breeding already existed there. The native practices were very specific. They featured a whole hierarchy of shepherds. Colonial chroniclers recorded in their stories the existence of certain animals that had been incorporated by the Indians into their everyday life, giving these animals names based on the similarities they showed with the European ones, as they often did with most of the new things they found in the Americas. For example, when they saw the *camelidae* from the New World they called them *carneros del Perú* (Peru's rams) or *carneros de la Tierra* (rams of the land), because they produced wool as well as the rams from the Old World did; they considered certain mute canines without hair to be "dogs," and certain web-footed birds that lived mainly in lands below 1,200 meters (4,000 feet) to be "ducks."

Camelidae

These distant relatives of camels are the llama, vicuña, alpaca, and guanaco. The former three had all been tamed by the natives, while the last one was a wild animal they usually hunted. They all dwelled in the Andean region and endured domestication not only to become beasts of burden, but also to serve as a source of wool and meat.

The llama (*Lama glama*) was bred by the Incas, who were known to have been shepherds. This practice allowed them to be promoted up to a high social standing, as those who carried out pasturage activities were organized in a hierarchy that ranged from simple herders to pasturage chiefs—the latter enjoying great prestige. These animals were considered to be holy and were often sacrificed in religious ceremonies, but they were also used as a source of meat—called *charqui* once salted and dried—and as beasts of burden. The wool they produced was not of excellent quality and was only used to make ponchos for the community. Due to the strict organization that characterized the Inca Empire, llama sacrifices required previous special authorization of the Inca emperor; those who infringed this rule were harshly punished.

The alpaca (*Lama pacos*) is said to have originated in the Andes near Lake Titicaca (between Peru and Bolivia), although they are nowadays found in other highlands of Peru and Bolivia. Whereas the llama used to be the Incas' beast of burden of choice, the alpaca was its main source for fiber production. While the llama prefers living in dry, arid, and not extremely cold environments, the alpaca needs to live in humid and even swampy cold areas endowed with fresh pastures. Alpacas are shorn when they reach two years of age—an activity that is always carried out during the rainy season, as this is the time of the year when their fleece is the cleanest. Alpaca wool is so fine that there were unsuccessful attempts to transfer this species to Spain during colonial times. Other attempts were also made in later times—in the middle of the nineteenth century—to acclimatize alpacas in Australia, but they were not successful either. Alpaca wool has been one of Peru's most important export items since 1836, when the Englishman Titus Salt discovered a way of manufacturing very fine cloth from this raw material. Like with the llama, the alpaca meat is dried and salted with culinary purposes. About 18 kilograms of usable meat can be obtained from a well-developed male specimen, while female ones only produce about 9 kilograms. But these are not the only purposes that alpacas can serve: their dried excrement can be used as fuel, which is of great importance, taking into consideration that firewood is scarce in the areas where they reside.

The vicuña (*Vicugna vicugna*)—very similar to the llama in terms of its physical appearance—is the smallest among the South American *camelidae* and also the most graceful and elegant. Its wool is as soft as silk and is of a light brown color that is known as "vicuña color." It resides in the Andean highlands, near the snowcapped mountains, up in the high, humid grasslands. While this delicate animal is used to prepare a highly prized cured meat, its preciousness comes from its wool. No wool is as fine and as delicate as that of the vicuña, which is why in the times of the Inca Empire only the emperor and his family could wear clothes made from vicuña. During the Spanish domination and then the republican times, vicuñas became endangered due to the expansion of uncontrolled hunting, leading to successive banning of this practice and to the establishment of strict regulations for its processing.

The guanaco (*Lama guanicoe*) is the only species of the genus that has always lived in a wild state. Its habitat extends from the south of Ecuador down to Patagonia. The guanaco is the tallest South American four-legged animal (approximately 1.1 meters or 3.6 feet). However, the higher the land it inhabits, the shorter the size of the specimen. Guanaco is not only known for its meat, which is used for culinary purposes, but also for its skin, which serves in the production of blankets. Its wool is also used to make certain fabrics, and even its bones are used to produce a great variety of objects.

The Mute Dog

When the Spanish arrived in South America, they realized that some indigenous tribes—especially those living in lands below 1,200 meters (4,000 feet)—had small four-legged animals they raised near their rooms and fattened up for culinary purposes as if they were piglets. These animals had no hair and did not bark; they only howled. According to the chronicles, the Spanish conquerors were soon enthusiasts of this little animal's meat, clearly contributing to its rapid and definitive extinction. The disappearance of this species led many people to doubt whether these *gozques* (as the Spaniards called them) had really existed, but modern archaeology has proved they did.

Cuy *or Guinea Pig*

These rodents (*Cavia porcellus*), similar to small rabbits, are referred to in the Andean region by the name *cuy* because of the brief squeals they produce when captured. They were domesticated all throughout the continent, from the warm Amazonian lands (where they were known as *acures*) to the cold, high Andean plateaus. They were very much prized for their meat, and even today are used for culinary purposes in rural areas, although they can also be found in certain urban restaurants, especially in Peru. Guinea pigs reproduce frequently and in large numbers, and have been a very important source of protein for South American farmers for centuries.

The Muscovy Duck

This web-footed bird (*Cairina moschata*)—also known as *pato amazónico* (Amazonian duck) or *pato real* (royal duck)—was very much prized for its

Man enjoys eating guinea pig and potatoes, Cuzco,
Peru. © TRIP/C. Rennie.

good-tasting meat. It had been domesticated by the Indians, and when
the Europeans arrived they immediately got used to eating it. The Europeans liked its meat so much that by the seventeenth century they had
already transferred it to France, where it was crossbred with the duck
of Nantes, as the South American bird was well known for its delicious
liver. The livers obtained in France today from this hybrid animal can be
said to owe their high quality to the sensory characteristics of the Muscovy duck's meat.

Domesticated Animals Brought from Abroad

The arrival of Europeans in the New World not only involved the conquest of ever-expanding territories, but also the transfer of breeding animals. As the conquerors entered the South American lands, they tried
not to totally depend on the foods they could get from the natives, so they
brought with them cattle and pig herds, as well as sheep and goat flocks.
These animals entered the continent with the members of the expeditions, who set aside some couples for future breeding and sacrificed others

for their own maintenance. It can be said that this livestock represented a kind of mobile pantry, which no doubt contributed a great deal to the success of many of the expeditions. It was impossible for the conquerors, incidentally, to prevent the escape of some cows or pigs when arriving in the new continent, which eventually went deeper into the scrublands and the jungle, changing their eating habits and becoming wild animals as a result of their new free condition. The fact is that the livestock introduced by the Spanish and the Portuguese reproduced so frequently and in such large numbers that they became a valuable possession to the colonists and even to the indigenous peoples who had undergone transculturation. The poultry brought by Europeans deserve a chapter to themselves. These birds also adapted to the new environment and reproduced abundantly. There is no doubt that the transfer of new animal species was one of the most successful undertakings of the Europeans in the New World, which meant a real revolution for the Indians.

Bovines

The Spanish and Portuguese conquerors' main source of power was certainly the use of firearms, horses, and dogs, thanks to which they could clearly assert their superiority over the Indians. But it is also true that the expeditionary forces could not survive and penetrate the new lands without food. In this sense, there is no doubt that livestock represented another pillar of the European domination.

There are records of cattle raising in the Caribbean coasts of South America—now Colombia and Venezuela—since the 1520s. In the 1530s cattle were brought to Ecuador and Peru, and then to the rest of the continent. It can be said that by the seventeenth century they were already spread throughout all South America, but especially in the different plains known as the Colombian-Venezuelan Llanos, the Brazilian Planicies and the Argentinean Pampas. Bovine herds proliferated so rapidly that, at the end of the eighteenth century, the Spanish and Portuguese together already owned some million head of cattle. It is particularly remarkable that livestock was not raised in farms in South America, but in complete liberty. Vast expanses of land could not be easily enclosed. When the cattle herders of the Llanos or of the Pampas needed to brand the animals, they had to start looking for them in the extensive savannas to round them up. The same procedure had to be followed before obtaining the different products from them. So it can be said that cattle raising in South America was carried out in liberty. Bovine herds were bred as a source of food, but mainly to use their hides. So during the time devoted to obtaining the various products from them, a great number were slaughtered to get many hides, and since the stockbreeders could only make use of part of the fresh meat and another part that they salted to produce jerky, many skinned animals remained abandoned in the fields, becoming the food of birds of prey and other carnivorous animals. Beef was never an expensive product during colonial and then republican times. Salted meat had to be desalted before its consumption, losing all its blood. This is why people became accustomed to having it fried or at least well done (as is the case of shredded meat). Some authors have noted that the hefty build and strength of many natives taking part in the independence armies had to do with their high meat consumption. As for the Colombian and Venezuelan cattle herders or *llaneros*, pasturage was very much similar to hunting, which enabled them to learn a number of stratagems to bring together all the animals, tame them, and then guide them to a specific place to complete their work. This is how they developed a kind of technique in which spears, hamstringing knives, and machetes played a key role. In the nineteenth century, when the *llaneros* were striving for independence, they applied this same technique to fight the troops that Spain had sent to suppress the independence movement, and, according to some people, this was a key factor in their victory.

Porcines

Pigs played an even more important role when brought by the conquerors, because they could be managed more easily. Their introduction in South America dates back to approximately 1509, and they reproduced as rapidly as cattle did. In the new lands, their diet changed. Their staple foods now included corn, cassava, and some tropical fruits like yellow *mombins* and guavas. This apparently led to an improvement in the quality of their meat, which was very soon considered to be even better than that produced in Europe. Many conquerors native to the province of Extremadura in Spain had been swineherders or had at least owned pigs, so they knew a lot about the breeding of this animal. Francisco Pizarro is perhaps the best-known example.

People make use of almost everything from swine, but what was mostly exploited in the Americas was their meat, and especially their fat. Lard (a product that is still very popular) was always used instead of olive oil in the new lands, because the olive tree—whose oil was very much used in Spain for cooking—did not flourish in most of South America. Other items that appeared as a result of the introduction of swine were sausages and cold meat. Preparation techniques were taught by both Spanish and Portuguese to the natives of the Americas. This is how the consumption of blood sausages, chorizos, spicy sausages, and other types of sausages and cold meat in general was spread throughout the whole continent, except for the Amazonian region.

Ovines and Caprines

Sheep were very much prized in the Iberian Peninsula, not only for their wool but also for their meat, which was generally preferred to that of cattle. Just like cows and pigs, sheep were brought to the South American continent from the beginning of the conquest, but they prospered mostly in the Andean region. They were introduced in large numbers; for example, Diego de Losada (Caracas's founder) brought with him 4,000 rams in 1567, while there had already been rams in Lima since around 1530. Thanks to the docility of this animal, the Indians of the region soon got used to breeding them, but due to this same quality they were easily seized by the wild animals of the Americas, hindering their prosperity to a large extent. The natives especially bred them in order to use them as the tributes they had to pay to the Spanish.

As for the goats, they were brought from the Canary Islands, Guinea, and Cape Verde. In the 1520s they had already been introduced, notably prospering in the Caribbean coasts. They were mostly appreciated as a source of soft leather (cordovans), which was very much used during colonial times. Compared with all the other four-legged animals that have been mentioned so far, goats were less important. Nevertheless, they became the most significant source of protein in the arid zones, thanks to their capacity to adapt to such environments.

Livestock was considered by the Iberian conquerors and colonizers to be their most precious possession, although the different meat types produced were not equally successful. As the old Hispanic saying goes:

The cow is noble;	La vaca, nobleza;
the sheep is wealth;	la oveja, riqueza;
the pig is a jewel;	el puerco, tesoro;
the goat is your help.	la cabra, socorro.

Poultry

Cocks and hens were also brought by Europeans in their expeditions to the Americas. At first, breeding poultry was not an easy task; they required a lot of attention, as they were frequently attacked by predatory animals. The indigenous people soon accepted them and started to breed them—also as a resource with which they would pay the tributes imposed by the conquerors. They spread throughout the whole continent, including the Amazonian region, where they can still be found. The high value of their meat was strongly related to the fact that corn kernels became their staple food when they arrived on the South American continent. These birds played a very important role in the colonists' diet. Their eggs had always been a key ingredient of the peninsular cuisine, which could be maintained thanks to the breeding of these animals in the Americas. Even the cocks—which were partly devoted to fights—were also famous for the substance they would give to broths when they were very old.

During the expeditions to trade slaves, the guinea fowl (*Numida meleagris*) was also transferred to South America, which many African slaves ended up breeding with much dedication in the new lands.

Another fowl that eventually played a significant role in the South American cuisine was the turkey. This bird was native to Central and North America and called *guajolote* by Mexicans. It was brought by the conquerors to Europe and, both there and then in North America, was subjected to a special type of breeding that produced high quantities of meat. This "developed" turkey was introduced in South America during the nineteenth century, becoming subject to breeding, although to a much lesser extent than hens.

ATTITUDES TOWARD FOOD

The main consequence of the cultural mixing was the predominance of the Spanish and the Portuguese languages, as well as of these peoples' customs and of the Catholic religion. However, the myths and superstitions of the Indians and the Africans did not totally disappear. The sobriety of the natives always contrasted with the Europeans' tendency to eat a lot. Eating with the family and showing a sense of Iberian hospitality became habits, which then began to fade in the twentieth century due to the social changes brought about by the ever-intensifying urban-development process.

The Religious Factor

The conquest of the New World by the Spanish and the Portuguese was not only aimed at achieving political domination. Since the beginning, it was proclaimed that its fundamental motive would be the replacement of the indigenous peoples' religious beliefs with the Catholic religion, or, as was commonly stated in the source material of colonial times, "the extirpation of idolatry from the Indians." The conqueror's sword entered the new lands along with the priest's or the missionary's cross. The Europeans were imbued with the idea of saving the souls of those gentiles and spared no effort to do so. They not only had to destroy temples and idols, but also had to teach their languages—Spanish and Portuguese—if they wanted to be successful in their evangelization. They certainly had to be able to communicate with the new subordinates in order to transmit to them their beliefs as well as the instructions observed by Christians. The missionaries made notable efforts to learn the indigenous languages and create catechisms to teach Christianity to the neophytes of the New World, but the final goal had always been that the natives would learn the languages of the conquerors. So their task was twofold: to teach them how to read and write, and to spread the Christian gospel.

All the priests' zeal was not enough to eradicate the religious beliefs of the South American Indians: the lands were too vast, the settlements too far from one another, the apostles preaching the religion too scarce, and the old beliefs of the indigenous peoples too deeply rooted. The contingent of people that had to be converted to Catholicism increased when large numbers of African slaves—who were also pagans and had their own religious beliefs—began to be transported to the Americas. During the domination practiced by the Spanish and the Portuguese in South America, the official religion of the Europeans coexisted with the many religions of the natives and the Africans. The latter continued to be practiced secretly or surreptitiously during Catholic religious ceremonies they pretended to accept. The Indians and the Africans looked at the images of the different Catholic saints thinking of their own traditional deities, and when the missionaries taught them to worship, they would practice it thinking of a pagan god instead of a saint. An example would be the slaves in Brazil—mostly from the African Yoruba culture—who identified Jesus with Obatala, Our Lady of the Rosary with Yemanya, Saint John the Baptist with Shango, and other saints with other deities of their own.

Myths, Superstitions, and Taboos of the Indigenous People

Before Columbus's arrival there was a great variety of religions in the Americas, most of which considered certain foods to be holy. Among the indigenous populations animism prevailed, which was based on the belief that the different elements of nature possessed particular spirits that had to be respected and to which offerings should be made. From the chronicles, it is known that in the Andean region potatoes and corn were considered to have their own gods, while the origins of their cultivation had been surrounded by a number of legends. On the one hand, the fertility of plants was a main concern in the religion of the Andean peoples. There existed, for example, the "Corn Mothers"—called *saramama* by the Incas—as well as the "fields' guards," who were in charge of farming the land, but whose role was not only a practical but also a religious one. They had to refrain from consuming salt and hot pepper and from having sexual relations with their wives on the days they had to work the land. On the other hand, almost all the tribes spread throughout the immense Amazonian basin believed—and there are some ethnic groups in those territories that still believe—that there was a kind of deity among hunter peoples, which they called "lord of beasts" in their different languages. They still believed that each animal species that was a hunting target had a kind of protective spirit. In addition, hunters had certain taboos: the prohibition to grill their own seized prey is the most common example.

In the Andean region, many ceremonies related to agriculture involved individual or collective offerings of different types of food, like that of *chicha*, as they believed it would foster the land's fertility.

The Arrival of Christianity: Fasting, Prohibition of Overindulgence, and Exclusion

The conquerors' religion entailed a great number of rules and practices related to food. Of great significance were the fasting precepts that had to be observed in certain times of the year, for example during Lent, or every Friday the whole year. In the Spanish literature of the fifteenth century there are many examples of such eating prohibitions, while at the same time there is the tendency to overindulgence or greed, which was considered to be a mortal sin. The Spanish peoples who lived during the Columbian times have usually been regarded as frugal, but it is very probable that they actually had no alternative and that they did not live that way voluntarily. Food was not particularly plentiful in the Iberian Peninsula during the fifteenth and sixteenth centuries. This situation changed for Europeans when they arrived in the New World, founded cities, established farms and haciendas, and obtained so much food they could give free rein to the satisfaction of their hunger.

The three main pillars of the Christians' diet and religious liturgy were wheat, grapevines, and olives. When they arrived in the Americas, and after a great number of attempts, they found it unfortunate that those cultures could not be transplanted in the whole South American region, but only in a small part of it, particularly in the lands with cold weather. The fact that these traditional European cultures did not prosper in many parts of the continent did not affect the conception the conquerors had of them, as they continued to consider them superior to those typical of the Americas, like corn and cassava. They never thought that corn and cassava could replace the European cultures within the context of religion; preparing the host—a key element of the holy mass—with corn or cassava flour was prohibited. The traditional beverages of the New World were likewise never considered possible substitutes for wine in the celebration of this religious sacrament.

In Europe, Christians were allowed to eat aquatic animals such as fish or shellfish during periods of abstinence. This practice continued to be carried out in South America, but the range of aquatic animals extended to include amphibians, as is the case of *carpincho* or *chigüire* (capybara), which made this religious eating restriction easier to bear. It is also worth mentioning that the conquerors benefited from the so-called Bull of the Holy Crusade, which was a papal permission to eat meat and dairy products without major restrictions. As the religious authorities considered the conquering practices to be related to the dissemination of the faith, the procedures applied were similar to those that had been carried out by the Europeans in the Holy War or Crusade of the Middle Ages to recover the Holy Sepulcher and expand the Christian faith among the unbelieving Muslims. Europeans also brought to South America their discriminatory views on the Jews. The Christians were heavy pork consumers, which differentiated them from the Jews. They were proud of this food habit and were suspicious of anybody who rejected ham or bacon. To be able to keep everything in order, they transferred to the New World the Inquisition practices aimed not only at prosecuting heresy and witchcraft, but also at ensuring the observation of the fast and abstinence precepts.

During the time of the Catholic kingdom, the conquerors and colonists that set sail for the Americas eventually imposed many of the European beliefs on the emerging societies of the New World. It was considered, for example, that passing the salt shaker from hand to hand would bring bad luck, while giving another person a knife would sever a relationship.

Religious Blending

The different beliefs of Indians, Europeans, and Africans were blended in the South American societies. A gaucho (cattle herder of the Argentinean Pampas) who was very far from any settlement would cross himself and say a number of prayers before eating his vegetable and meat stew in order to drive away any evil from his food, believing that no food could be eaten if it had not been blessed. There are also traces of the ceremonies carried out in Peru and Bolivia during the times of the Inca Empire. Some examples would be the rites performed in August and May to celebrate sowing and harvesting, respectively. These ceremonies not only involve mass celebration, but also traditional pre-Columbian offerings to the land.

Food Habits

According to the conquest chroniclers, one of the causes of the decrease in the indigenous population was the conquerors' imposition of their food habits. Such intervention has been considered lethal, not only because of the changes in the native diet components, but also because of the incorporation of the Spanish habit of eating three times a day and in large quantities, when the Indians had always been moderate in their eating habits. There are plenty of testimonies on the conquerors' lavish meals, in which they consumed in one or two days what would have fed the Indians for weeks or months. However, the Indians' sobriety should not be taken for granted. Even though according to the source material available they ate in moderation, in the sense that they did not commit overindulgence, all their physical features indicate that their diet was a very balanced one and that they fed themselves properly. They had shiny hair and healthy teeth, and Indian women gave birth easily without the help of midwives. Once conquered, the natives were deprived of their free access to food to a great extent and had to comply with the rules imposed by the invaders who had seized their lands. This is the reason why they started to feel hungry and to steal fruits and edible animals, which explains in turn why the Europeans started to brand them as insatiable- and thieving people.

It was said before that those who came to the Americas in the discovery and conquest times had a sort of pent-up hunger that made them display overindulgence in food and drink when they became aware of all the food riches the New World offered to them, which were cultivated and bred by the natives or the slaves for them. Beef especially was so abundant in most of the new lands that it was within everyone's reach due to its ridiculous price. Thus, a meat-based diet became a habit that imposed itself as a pattern, which prevails even today, although the great majority cannot follow it because of their economic conditions. There is still a widespread idea that a meal without meat should not be called a meal.

The family was the essential core in the Iberian tradition. When the new cities were founded and the houses were built in the European way, the house of the family continued to be the appropriate place for the meals. Families were large and not only comprised father, mother, and children, but also grandparents, in-laws, and close friends—all taking part in the food habit of choice. Europeans, especially Spaniards, had a strong sense of hospitality, which also used to be a manifestation of wealth or of an acceptable living standard. This feature did not vanish when they crossed the ocean. The less privileged copied such behavior, as it would apparently make them look in some way like the wealthy. Even today, any tourist or traveler will be received in any humble South American household with a warm welcome, where they will be offered a *cafecito* (a small cup of coffee), a maté, or any other little snack regardless of the hosts' social standard.

The accelerated urban-development process had an influence on those patriarchal customs. The rapid pace of the city life, which has partly dismantled the family, has brought about a decline of this traditional hospitality. In the city, life tends to be anonymous and individualism eventually prevails; people need to go to work, and the houses are often left empty. Food prices have spiraled in those mostly underdeveloped economies, which is one reason why South Americans are less friendly than in the past.

NOTES

1. George McClelland Foster, *Culture and Conquest: America's Spanish Heritage* (Chicago: Quadrangle Books, 1960), p. 229.

2. Joseph de Acosta, *Historia natural y moral de las Indias*, vol. 1 (1590; reprint, Madrid: Ramón Anglés, 1894), p. 250.

3. José Nuix y Perpiñá, *Reflexiones imparciales sobre la humanidad de los españoles en las Indias*, vol. 2 (1780; reprint, Madrid: Ediciones Atlas, 1944), pp. 174–75. This work was originally published in Venice in Italian as *Riflessioni imparziali sopra l'umanitá degli spagnuoli nell'Indie*. The original text in Spanish: "Las artes y la industria, por medio de los españoles, fueron a domiciliarse entre aquellas gentes. Proveyóseles inmediatamente de instrumentos para el cultivo de la tierra y para las manufacturas más útiles, y se poblaron los desiertos de los animales necesarios para la agricultura, para el alimento y para otros usos. La tierra comenzó a verse cubierta de nuevos frutos, y el campo correspondía ventajosamente a los deseos y a las esperanzas de los nuevos cultivadores. Abandonados ya los bosques,

las cazas penosas y las pescas arriesgadas, en vez de chozas habitaron en albergues cómodos y sanos; *alimentáronse de comida más nutritiva, más sabrosa y regular* [italics added]; cubrieron su desnudez y, finalmente, se avergonzaron de su antiguo estado.

2

Major Foods and Ingredients

The mixing process that gave birth to the South American society called *criolla* preserved the major foods used by the Indians since pre-Columbian times (potatoes, corn, beans, and cassava) and other native ingredients (hot pepper, vanilla). However, the presence of the Europeans led to the incorporation of new food sources brought from the Old World and even from Asia and Africa, which became part of the culinary heritage of South Americans. The most important contributions were grains (such as wheat and rice), spices, sugar cane, some fruits such as citrus, and especially meat and poultry. The South American cuisine was extraordinarily enriched by the great variety of edible species taken from the sea or the rivers. The incorporation of the different livestock species brought by the conquerors resulted in the manufacture of the main dairy products. As for drinks, native beverages such as *chicha* ended up coexisting with wine, coffee, and, more recently, carbonated beverages.

STAPLE FOODS

Beans

Beans are native to the Americas. Botanists gave them the name *Phaseolus*—a Latin word derived from the Greek word *phaselos*, meaning "small basket." This name was given to them because this plant contained the beans in a sort of receptacle. Even though all South Americans know very well what the word *frijol* (bean) refers to, this is not the name used colloquially in all countries of the continent. In Argentina, for example, they call it *poroto,* and in other parts the name has suffered some changes and resulted in words like *fréjol* or *frisol.* The cultivation of this legumi-nous plant in the New World dates back to earlier than 6000 B.C., as ar-chaeological remains have testified in Mexico and Peru. Bean crops were spread by the indigenous populations from these two key points to the rest of the continent, so when the Europeans arrived in the New World this plant was grown almost everywhere. It had always been present in the pre-Columbian diet, along with corn, which resulted in the aforementioned positive nutritional effects.

There are more than 100 different varieties of beans, which are differ-ent in shape, color, taste, and nutritional values. In general terms, only some of them are eaten in South America nowadays—most of them being kidney-shaped with colors ranging from white to black. In Venezuela, black beans receive the name *caraotas,* which are heavily consumed in this country as they are a key ingredient of a number of typical dishes, such as *pabellón, sopa de caraotas,* and *carabinas* (a sort of corn-made ta-male filled with beans). Black beans are not only used to prepare savory dishes, but also sweet ones.

Due to their high protein value, black beans can substitute for meat, which is the reason why they have been called "the poor man's meat." Ac-cording to a number of research studies, the iron they contain is much less assimilable. The nutritional value of red beans is similar to that of black beans, although they taste differently.

Capsicum: From Sweet to Hot

The royal chronicler Peter Martyr d'Anghiera announced, in his de-lightful Renaissance style, one of the many novelties of the New World. His story recounts how the discoverers, in their first return journey to Spain, had brought with them certain elongated and rough vegetable capsules of different colors that were hotter than peppers. This is how the capsicum or "the pepper from the Indies"—as it was then called—arrived in the Old World. The Swedish botanist Linnaeus gave it the name *Capsicum frutescens,* while the Nahuatl called it *chilli* and the Que-chua *uchu,* but the Taino word *aji* was the one that prevailed and remained for posterity as a South Americanism, as was the case of many other Taino words. This discovery enriched the range of spices known in the Old World and, at the same time, justified Columbus's sailing of the unknown ocean looking for the spices of the East. The explorer had not found the famous pepper, but he discovered this new spice from the Americas instead, which soon won over the Europeans. The use of capsicum quickly spread throughout Spain, because by 1565 Nicolás Monardes—a famous physician from Seville who showed great interest in the products of the Americas—said that there was no vegetable garden without it. He also said that capsicum was used in all stews and pots, exalting its enormous economic value, because black pepper was much more expensive, while the cost of capsicum was only the effort of sowing it. This member of the *Solanaceae* family, whose cultivation in South America dates back to more than 7,000 years, was soon as successful in other European countries as it had been in Spain, from where its cultivation spread to Italy and other parts of the continent. Since the sixteenth century, this hot fruit from the Americas has become famous, and it eventually penetrated all cuisines of the Old World, appearing as an ingredient in many culinary preparations. However, there was also a variety of this fruit that was not hot, but sweet. The latter sweet variety was bigger than the hot variety and constituted the origin of the Spanish pepper or *pimiento*.

The hot variety is very much used in Ecuador, Peru, Bolivia, and the Amazonian region as an ingredient of a number of dishes, whereas in Venezuela, Chile, and Argentina the sweet variety is preferred. In these latter countries, each person adds the peppery flavor to his or her own food, to taste, using a capsicum sauce container called an *ajicero*.

Cassava or Manioc

Botanists classed this root vegetable as a member of the *Euphorbiaceae* family and called it *Manihot esculenta*, honoring the original word the Guarani people used to refer to it: *mandiog*. Cassava had been grown in the continent as a means of sustenance for many centuries before the arrival of the Europeans. There are basically two varieties of cassava: the sweet one (eaten as a vegetable) and the bitter one. Although the latter contains a poisonous substance (hydrocyanic acid), it was transformed into a food thanks to the inventiveness of South American Indians. They changed death into life, so to speak, as they enabled this root to be eaten in the form of bread (called *casabe*) or starch (known as *tapioca* or *mañoco*). In almost all South America, including Brazil, cassava is known as *mandioca*, but in Venezuela and Colombia it receives the name *yuca*—a word of West Indian origin, specifically from the language of the Taino natives.

Some specialists point out that the methods used to process bitter cassava originated in the Lower Orinoco River, where archaeological remains have been found as evidence of their application, dating back to the early first millennium B.C. Nevertheless, according to other specialists, those methods originated in the region of the Magdalena River in Colombia.

Europeans brought cassava from South America to Africa in the sixteenth century, where it flourished so well that it became a staple food and made many Africans believe it is native of their continent. The slaves taken to South America in the seventeenth century and in the following centuries already knew cassava when they arrived in the New World, so they simply reinforced the general consumption of this root vegetable.

Because there are two types of cassava—bitter and sweet—it is very important to be able to differentiate between them when shopping, as there is no clear difference in shape or color. This is obviously dangerous to some extent, because a mistake could lead to food poisoning. Experienced buyers already know how to differentiate them, especially because sweet cassava has two easily removable skins—a thinner outer one and a fleshier inner one—while the skins of bitter cassava are thicker and more difficult to remove. This is why shoppers usually break the tuber in two, in order to be able to identify them, which is a very common practice in the South American markets. It is also remarkable that sellers not only tolerate this from buyers, but typically break the vegetable themselves for display.

Corn

It has been said, and rightly so, that South Americans are the people of maize. This grain is certainly a symbol of their cuisine, just like rice is an Asian icon or wheat represents Europe—although according to modern statistics wheat consumption is quantitatively higher than that of corn in South America. Corn (Zea mays) has always played a main role in the South American cookbooks, overshadowing the other ingredients, thanks to the great number and wide variety of dishes in which it appears.

Chroniclers called it "the wheat from the Indies" in an attempt to express how important it was for the sustenance of the New World's inhabitants. Transcribing the term used by Tainos, they also called it Ma-Hiz—a name that quickly spread and supplanted the other names that had been used in the region to refer to this plant during pre-Columbian times. The Aztecs had called it centli or cintli, while the Incas had called it zara.

This fleshy grain is the base of almost all the regional dishes, ranging from the arepa (the traditional bread of Venezuela and part of Colombia), to the various pies, cakes, and mazamorras (corn-based milky puddings), including the Ecuadorian, Peruvian, and Chilean bollos (bread buns) and tamales, the *pamonhas* from southern Brazil, and beverages such as the *atoles* (hot corn drinks) and the *chicha*. The annual per-capita corn consumption in South America amounted to 23.7 kilograms in 2001.

According to specialists:

Fifty to 80% of the niacin in corn cannot be assimilated by the human body; consequently, people whose diet is comprised almost solely of corn often suffer from pellagra, a disease caused by a niacin-deficient diet, which affects the central nervous system, the digestive system, the skin, and the mucous lining of the mouth. The ancestral practice of adding lime, caustic soda, or ashes to corn was an instinctive way of compensating for the nutritional deficiencies of this cereal, as the addition of these substances makes the niacin in corn assimilable.[1]

This nutritional benefit used to be reinforced by the consumption of beans—a staple in the pre-Columbian diet—which explains why Indians and their descendants now have never suffered from pellagra.

Potatoes

The potato (*Solanum tuberosum*) is said to have originated in the Andean highlands, particularly in the basin of Lake Titicaca, from where it began to spread throughout the rest of the Andean region during pre-Columbian times. The European conquerors and colonizers eventually helped to disseminate its use in the rest of South America, so that by the seventeenth century it was a common food beyond the Andean zone. The Spanish chroniclers of the conquest who tasted the potatoes called them *turmas* or *criadillas* (truffles) at the beginning, as their shape was very similar to that of the animals' testicles. However, in Spanish America and the Canaries, this tuber was then called *papa*—a word from the Quechua language. In Europe, Spaniards called it *patata*, as they confused it with the name of another tuber that was also native to the Americas, namely the *batata* (sweet potato; *Ipomoea batata*), which then gave rise to the English name "potato." In Peru and Bolivia, there are hundreds of different varieties of this *Solanaceae* family member of many different sizes and colors, most of which used to be eaten by the indigenous population. This root vegetable was immediately accepted by the conquerors, but it took at least 100 years for it to be adopted in Europe, where it underwent a number of delicate treatments that resulted in new potato varieties that differed from those of the New World in shape and texture. Some of these new varieties are now paradoxically imported from South America.

Potatoes have been one of the most important South American staple foods for time immemorial. Although the ways to prepare it have changed with time, traditional recipes still coexist in the South American cuisine with the now very famous French fries. In the Peruvian highlands, potatoes are also consumed in the form of *chuno* or *chuño* (potato flour), which is obtained by freezing and drying potatoes through exposure to the elements. Out of the 3,000 existing potato varieties, around 100 are used today for human consumption.

Llapingachos (Ecuador)

- 2 pounds potatoes
- 1 onion, finely chopped
- 1/2 pound white cheese, crumbled
- 2 tablespoons butter
- 1 teaspoon salt

Sauce

- 1/2 pound peanuts, toasted and ground
- 1/2 cup milk
- 3 tablespoons onion, finely chopped
- 3 tablespoons butter

Wash, peel, and boil potatoes until tender. Mash them and mix them with a tablespoon of butter and a little bit of salt. Sauté the onions. Add the crumbled cheese to the onions. Shape the mashed potatoes into small balls and stuff them with the cheese-based mixture. Seal and brown them. Sprinkle with the peanut sauce.

Sauce. Sauté the onions in a tablespoon of butter. Add the peanuts and the milk. Cook over medium heat until it thickens. Serve all the fried balls and the sauce in separate bowls. (6 servings)

OTHER IMPORTANT FOODS AND INGREDIENTS

Beverages

Native

A key South American beverage is *chicha*. Although the first documents recording the use of this word date back to the very early sixteenth century, etymologists still disagree on its origin. According to some, this term was first used by the Panama's Cuna Indians; others say it was an Arawak or Otomí term; yet others even base their arguments on the opinion of the accredited Spanish chronicler Gonzalo Fernández de Oviedo, who considers *chicha* a Taino word. In any case, it is particularly remarkable that even though this word was originally used to designate a fermented corn beverage, it was then also used to refer to beverages obtained from any grain. There are records of this word in the pages written by almost all the conquest and colonial chroniclers, and the corn-based type has been consumed since. There are different ways to prepare *chicha* depending on the region, but the method generally consists of grinding the corn kernels, adding *guarapo de piña* (sweet pineapple juice), and then fermenting the mixture. According to some chroniclers, this latter task was traditionally entrusted to the old women, who chewed the preparation and then spit it out in a jug in order to speed up the fermentation process. Some particular Spaniards were somewhat disgusted when they first saw this practice. They had no reason for rejecting this method, though, as it had also been applied in a number of regions in Spain to prepare the famous *aioli* sauce. In fact, women chewed the garlic cloves, which were then gradually mixed with oil and stirred together. This produced the well-known emulsion the inhabitants of the Iberian Peninsula have been preparing and using as a sauce, creating real culinary delicacies for time immemorial. Corn-based *chicha* was produced by most of the South American Indian tribes. In more recent times, its preparation and consumption have been confined to the Andean region and the areas inhabited by the surviving pre-Columbian ethnic groups. But, since long ago, *chicha* has also been prepared with rice instead of corn, resulting in a beverage that has been industrially manufactured in some countries like Venezuela and Colombia.

Mate (maté) is a bitter and greenish infusion or tea made from the leaves of a tree native to South America called *Ilex paraguariensis*, *Ilex mate*, and *Ilex curitibensis*. It is mainly consumed in the southern zone of the continent, in Argentina, southern and southwestern Brazil, Paraguay, Uruguay, and central and southern Chile, although it is also consumed in some parts of Peru and Bolivia. *Mate* is a Guarani word that was used to designate the gourd (a member of the *Curcubitaceae* family and scientifically known as *Lagenaria vulgaris*) that served as a container for the beverage. The Spaniards Hispanicized this word by designating the drink with the name of the container. By calling the infusion matter *yerba-mate*, as it is known in the Spanish-speaking countries, it is being designated with the name of two different botanical species.

In pre-Hispanic times, it was grown by the Guarani Indians, who introduced it to the other ethnic groups, like the Quechua and the Chiriguano indigenous peoples.

The Spanish and the Portuguese appreciated and adopted this beverage, which had been referred to during the eighteenth century in Spanish as *thé de las misiones* (missions tea), *thé del Paraguay* (Paraguay tea), *thé del Sur* (tea of the south), or *thé de los jesuitas* (Jesuits' tea), and in Portuguese as *erva de palo* (stick herb) or *congonha verdadeira* (real *congonha*).

This stimulant and invigorating beverage is consumed in different forms depending on the region. Bitter or sweet, it is in any case sipped through a special straw called a *bombilla*, which is made of silver or other less valuable metals.

As for cocoa, it shall be said first that each period of time in history has featured a specific beverage that characterizes it as a whole. The seventeenth century, the Italian Seicento, was marked by chocolate, which settled in the European courts and abbeys once introduced by the Spaniards. It was a dense, sweet, and aromatic foam-covered potion—in other words, noble. The history of its consumption can be divided into two long phases: the first one—ranging from the pre-Hispanic to the early nineteenth century—marked by the consumption of the beverage (cocoa), and the second one, in which the production of a solid (chocolate) from the cacao plant began. Nowadays, the consumption of the solid product of the *Theobroma* tree prevails over that of the beverage. The seeds of this plant are industrially processed to produce bar chocolate that is sold in the form of candies or desserts of various types. By contrast, the word *chocolate* only referred to the delicious beverage during colonial times.

Of Foreign Origin

Even though coffee is native to Asia and was only introduced in South America in the second half of the eighteenth century, when the coffee plantations started to prosper—especially during the nineteenth century in Venezuela, Colombia, and Brazil—the infusion it produced displaced some native beverages like cocoa, taking root in the South American food habits to such an extent that coffee can be considered a typical beverage. However, most of the South American coffee production is exported. Due to their habit of using the diminutive form of words, South Americans very soon baptized this beverage as the *cafecito* or the *cafezinho*.

By the year 2001, the annual per-capita coffee consumption was 1.7 kilograms, less than half the equivalent in the United States (4 kilograms).

Carbonated beverages, the invention of which dates back to the late eighteenth century, did not arrive in South America until the second half of the nineteenth century, with the establishment of the first specialized industries. Their dissemination basically took place during the following century, when refrigeration and ice production had spread. Due to their refreshing nature, they became very popular, especially in the tropical zone. The fact that some plants had established in South America for the production of carbonated beverages did not affect the imports, which had been carried out mainly from the United States. As they became popular in the region and as some of the countries adopted industrialization policies during the twentieth century, many transnational enterprises that produced these beverages established their plants in the region to spread their own brands.

However, new versions of carbonated beverages have been produced in South America, taking into consideration people's likes and giving them typical regional names. In Peru, for example, there is a yellow-colored lemon-flavored type of carbonated beverage called Inca Cola. Something similar happened in Brazil, where guarana (*Paullinia cupana* H.B.K.) was used as a flavoring agent of a carbonated soft drink. The seeds of this woody plant native to the Amazonian region were first used by the Indians to make a substance with which they would prepare one of the most stimulant beverages that has existed—as it contains three times as much caffeine as coffee does. The consumption of this guarana-based soda has spread in Brazil since the 1970s, while it has also been exported to other South American countries.

Beer used to be imported during the nineteenth century. It was not until late in that century and in the early twentieth century that beer industries began to be established in South America. The first beer plants were founded in Peru in 1863, in Ecuador and Uruguay in 1866, in Brazil in 1888, in Colombia and Venezuela in 1889, in Paraguay in 1894, in Chile in 1896, and in Argentina in 1908. Beer's low alcohol content, its refreshing nature, and its reasonable price were key factors for its rapid spread in the South American region, especially where there was no production of wine. The beer industry has developed a great deal, especially in Brazil and Venezuela. Many types of beer are produced, from *cerveza negra* (dark beer) to *cerveza rubia* (lager), and from bitter to the pilsner type, including a number of other smooth or light classes. By the year 2001, the annual per-capita beer consumption was 36.2l—lower than that of the United States (89.5l), though. Beer marketing has been so successful and has developed to such an extent that two of the largest South American transnational corporations are devoted to this industry, exporting large quantities of this beverage to the United States.

The main South American producers of wine are Argentina, Chile, Brazil, Bolivia, Peru, and Uruguay. Argentina produces the largest volumes but is the country with the lowest export rates, as it consumes a ninth of its own production. This country is followed by Chile, which is Latin America's largest wine-exporting nation. This country has been capable of quickly renewing its wine industry and taking great care in the marketing of its wines, which are currently well known around the world. Wines produced in the other aforementioned South American countries are consumed domestically and lack the reputation of the Argentinean and Chilean wines. In Argentina and Chile, unlike in the equatorial countries, wine is a popular beverage consumed by everyone—from farmers and workers to great magnates. This vast wine culture is not seen in the rest of the nations of the continent, where wine has been consumed on a small scale and only by the middle classes living in the urban areas.

Condiments

Salt

The use of salt in South America during pre-Columbian times was not homogeneous. It played a very weak role, for example, in the Amazonian Basin, where it was replaced by capsicum, or even in regions where it abounded, like in the Goajira Peninsula (Venezuela and Colombia). In other regions, it was obtained from different sources (i.e., from salt mines, the sea, or mineral deposits). Some mainland indigenous peoples did not use it as an ingredient to prepare their foods, but rather as a kind of complement that each person would use to taste when eating. Some Indians would have a piece of salt near them at mealtimes, which they would lick from time to time.

The presence of the Dutch in the Caribbean in the seventeenth century, where they established and took control of the Curaçao, Bonaire, and Aruba islands, and, for a considerable period of time, also the Araya Peninsula in Venezuela, was not only aimed at playing a role within the Caribbean trade market (which they did through smuggling), but also at taking possession of the salt mines of Araya, which would grant them a continuous provision of the precious mineral, without which they would not have been able to develop their economy, based on the production of salted herring, butter, and cheese. South Americans, especially the dwellers of the Andean region, do not use much salt as an ingredient when cooking or eating. Yet their consumption of this mineral remains high, as they still eat salted meat and fish.

Sugar

The transfer of sugar plantations to the New World was based on the development of the sugar industry carried out by the Spanish and the Portuguese in the islands they had colonized in the Atlantic Ocean, namely the Canaries, the Azores, and São Tomé. Sugar cane first arrived in the Caribbean, brought by Christopher Columbus from the Canary Islands in his second voyage of 1493. In 1496 sugar was shipped to Europe for the first time from the Spanish island of Santo Domingo. Despite the express will of the Spanish Crown to expand sugar cultivation throughout the islands, it was in the mainland where the sugar industry mostly developed. The slaves brought to the New World to work in the mines of the Crown soon started to work in the sugar plantations, which prospered in Paraguay, as well as in the Pacific coasts and the fertile valleys of South America, the mainland production beating the insular one.

Although the exact date of the sugar cane's arrival in Brazil is uncertain, by the year 1526 the Portuguese were already shipping large quantities of sugar to Lisbon. A century later, they were among the most important European suppliers of this sweetening substance produced in Brazil. Sugar factories underwent a considerable and constant evolution in this South American country, so that by the year 1683, 66 factories produced 2,700 tons of sugar that were transported by 40 ships to Europe, where the product stopped being a luxury good to become ever more affordable to the masses.

South Americans consumed unrefined sugar—commonly called *dulce* (sweet)—during colonial times, as the refining industry had been expressly banned by the peninsular authorities. The first modern refining factories were established in the continent in the nineteenth century. However, people continued using unrefined sugar. It is in fact an ingredient of many of the typical South American sweet and even some savory dishes.

Nowadays sugar is consumed both in its natural and in its refined form. The natural or noncentrifugal form is known in Venezuela as *papelón* or *panela*, in Argentina as *raspadura*, in Brazil as *rapadura*, and in Peru as *chancaca*. In 2001, the per-capita consumption of noncentrifugal sugar was 45.2 kilograms, while that of refined sugar was 3.5 kilograms.

Vinegar

Vinegar was brought to South America by the explorers and conquerors and soon started to be produced in the new lands during colonial times, although the vinegar arriving from Europe continued to be considered the best. The latter was called "vinegar of Castile," obviously alluding to the place where it was produced. Vinegar production was carried out without much effort, as wine or any other alcoholic beverage acidified when left exposed to the air. Balsamic vinegar is very famous today and has been imported to all the South American countries, although it is generally used only in the main cities.

Dairy Products

During the colonial Spanish domination, cow's milk consumption and at the same time the production of butter, whey and cream, and cheese spread throughout the region. Cheese was also obtained from goat's milk. Up-to-date sanitary laws are now enforced in all South American countries, where milk and dairy products are pasteurized everywhere, except for some small-scale farmhouse production units.

Up until the middle of the twentieth century, milk was usually delivered in the South American cities by a milkman, who would go from door to door announcing his presence by shouting, "*Lechero!*" (the Spanish word for "milkman"), sometimes sounding a cowbell and selling the milk that had been obtained from the cows that same morning. He would have it stored in metal containers (first of copper and then of aluminum) that held about 40 liters, which were commonly called *cántaros*. He used to carry these containers on a donkey or mule cart, and the neighbors would reach the milkman with their own vessels in order to have him fill them up with a small receptacle of about 1.5 liters of capacity called a *cántara* or *cantarilla*. This tradition is still practiced today in isolated rural areas, but now the metal containers have been replaced by plastic ones and the cart has been replaced by a motor vehicle.

Almost all dairy products are salty, because when they started to be produced in colonial times, the only method to preserve them was through salt. This explains why South Americans are accustomed to this taste. It is very difficult, for example, to find fresh cream (i.e., no salt) unless one is in a city.

South American cheeses are typically fresh (i.e., unripe) and produced with cow's milk. The amount of salt can vary from one cheese type to another, but this mineral is always present. There are different classes depending on their consistency, ranging from *cuajada* (curd) to the so-called *quesos duros* (hard cheeses). Nowadays they are industrially produced, but the small production units located in the country (not in the capitals) have not disappeared because of this. In certain regions, where goat raising plays an important role—as is the case of north-central and northwestern Venezuela or northern Peru—there are also cheese varieties that are produced from goat's milk, though always unripe. During the twentieth century, especially in the second half, South Americans started to produce a number of new cheese classes in an attempt to imitate some of the famous European cheeses such as Brie, Camembert, or Roquefort (native to France); the Parmesan cheese (from Italy); and some other lesser-known classes. The underlying purpose of trying to copy these foreign cheeses has been, from the very beginning, to stop or to reduce the imports of cheese and thus save the countries of the region money.

Dyes

Annatto

This dye (*Bixa orellana*) has been referred to with different names: *onoto*, *achote*, *achiote*, *bijo*, and *bija*. In the Guianas, Brazil, and Argentina it is called *urucu*. It is native to South America and is cultivated in warm tropical zones. The annatto tree is small and produces capsule-like fruits about 5 cm (two inches) in diameter, which open into two valves when dried to release the seeds. The indigenous communities of the Americas used it in different ways, but especially for body painting. It was rather late that annatto began to be referred to as a culinary ingredient in the equatorial Americas. The Iberian conquerors were accustomed to using saffron to dye certain foods like rice—a habit they had probably inherited from the Arabs. As they did not find any saffron in the New World, they started using annatto as a substitute. It was not only used to dye rice, but also many other dishes, such as the corn dough used to prepare some of the tamales, soups like the *ajiaco bogotano*, sausages, and even potato-based dishes. But it has also been used in South America to dye certain sweet dishes, for example as an ingredient in the caramel coating of certain dishes like the *coquitos* (Venezuelan small sweet balls). If used in excess, there is a risk that the food will get an overpowering taste by acquiring the annatto seed's flavor.

Palillo

Also called *azafrán*, *azafrán de raíz*, *azafrán quitense*, *quillocaspi*, *sauna*, and *azafrán de los Andes*, the *palillo* root (*Escobedia scabrifolia* R. and P.) was used by the Indians to color food yellow. It abounds in the Peruvian mountains and is widely used in this country to dye rice and certain sauces.

Fish

The South American region has been blessed by nature with regard to its fish repertoire, as it is endowed with a great variety of marine species from the two oceans bordering the continent and by the fauna riches of its rivers—particularly the Orinoco, the Amazon, and the Paraná. The pre-Columbian Indians showing the greatest interest in the sea products were those inhabiting the territory of what is now Peru. They also stood out for the creation of the most varied fish-based recipes. The arrival of the Europeans simply reinforced the general liking for fish, which eventually developed into a key feature of the resulting mixed society's cuisine.

Even though the fishing activity is nowadays carried out through modern trawlers, these coexist with a great number of small boats driven by fishermen, who are protected by the state and whose practices are considered to be friendlier to the environment than those of industrial fishing.

There is a preference for white-meat fish among South Americans, some maritime species being particularly appreciated, namely *pargo* (*Lutjanus* spp.), which is a kind of snapper; *mero* or grouper (*Epinephelus* spp.); *lenguado* (*Paralichthys adspersus*), which is a kind of sole; *pejerrey* or silverside (*Odontesthes regia regia* Humboldt); and *corbina* (*Ciluf gilberti*). They are followed by fish of darker meat like *carite* or mackerel (*Scomberomorus* spp.) and *cazón* or shark (*Carcharhinus* spp.). As for the freshwater fish living in the vast continental river network, there is high consumption along the rivers, but also a considerable proportion is salted and taken to the nearest urban markets. *Bagres* (catfish) are the most famous freshwater fish, which include a number of varieties—some of them rejected by the urban populations because of their reputation for living on unsavory scraps. The most coveted freshwater fish is probably the *Brachyplatistoma* genus, known in Venezuela as *valentón*, in the Guianas as *lau-lau*, in Brazil as *surubim*, and in Argentina as *surubí*.

As for crustaceans and mollusks, lobsters and oysters are the most famous within the gastronomical field. In order of importance—and prob-

Irapa man drying fish, Paria, Venezuela. © TRIP/M. Cerny.

ably due to their lower price—these are followed by crabs, river shrimp, mussels, clams, and scallops, as well as cephalopods such as octopuses and squid.

Fruits

Native

Avocado—baptized as *Persea gratissima* Gaertn. and also as *Persea americana* L.—is the fruit of a tree from the *Lauraceae* family, which is native to Central America and northern South America, where the greatest variety of its species and subspecies can be found. There are archaeological remains proving that it was first cultivated in 3,000 B.C. in the Peruvian coasts. Since the early days of the conquest, the Spanish conquerors praised the appearance and delicious taste of the fruit, which they compared to a pear. Martín Fernández de Enciso mentions the avocado in his *Suma de Geografía*, published in Seville in 1519. There are different names in the continent to refer to this fruit, namely *cura* or *curo*, used in Venezuela and in the Colombian Magdalena River region, and probably a word from the Chibcha language; *palta*, used in Ecuador, Peru, Bolivia, Chile, and Argentina, a name that apparently derived from the Ecuadorian Jivaran language and was then adopted by the Quechua language; *abacate*, used in

Brazil; and, last but not least, *aguacate*, a name resulting from the Nahuatl language that spread widely throughout South America.

This fruit was very popular during pre-Columbian times, when it was consumed raw without any special preparation. In northern Peru, the Indians would hold a party that lasted about a week to celebrate the ripening of the fruit. The youth would congregate in an open area; from here they would race to a nearby hill and try to catch and court the beloved women. This ceremony was a symbol that combined human fertilization with the search for the land's fertility. Since their arrival in South America, the Spanish and the Portuguese adopted the avocado and used it in new ways for culinary purposes, adding sugar, honey, or even vinegar and crushing it to make sauces. Today, the avocado has even been transformed into a dessert with a popular avocado-based ice cream prepared in Brazil.

The papaya was one of the first fruits discoverers and chroniclers found when they arrived in the Americas. It is known in Venezuela as *lechosa* and in Brazil as *mamão*. But the Europeans first called it *higuera de las Indias* (fig tree from the Indies), and from this inadequate name the botanist Linnaeus decided to name it *Carica papaya*. *Carica* was the Latin term for figs, while *papaya*, according to the laborious but challenging research carried out by lexicographers, seems to derive from the word *mapaya*, used by the Venezuelan Tamanaco Indians to designate this fruit.

Papayas are native to the New World, but it is not clear whether they originated in the Antilles, in Central America, or in South America. The papaya plant grows rapidly and is endowed with a hollow, nonwoody stem upon which there is a crown of large leaves divided into several lobes. The papaya tree can be "male" or "female." The fruit of the female is ovoid-shaped and has few seeds, while that of the male is elongated.

It is eaten fresh, either cut into pie-like or round slices, or into irregularly shaped pieces to be used in salads, as well as blended in shakes. Papayas have antidyspeptic properties, as scientific studies have demonstrated that its pulp has an enzyme called papain, which assists in transforming proteins and thus contributes to proper food digestion. Besides, papain (similar to pepsin) is used to tenderize beef. Agricultural workers have been aware of this property of papain since ancient times, wrapping tough meat with papaya leaves or cooking it with them.

Soursop, cherimoya, and the other members of the *Annonaceae* family amount to no less than 800 species. One of the most important genera in this family is known as *Annona*, which includes three fruits that are native to the intertropical regions of the American continent, namely soursop (*Annona muricata*), cherimoya (*Annona cherimola*), and sugar apple

(*Annona squamosa*). These three fruits have delighted a great number of palates with their white and fleshy pulp. The generic name *Annona* is derived from Latin and means the food or provisions for a whole year, thus symbolizing abundance. As for the word *cherimola*, etymologists debate on its Quechua or Quiche origins (meaning "fruit of cold land" in Quechua).

Cherimoya—native to Central America and then successfully acclimatized in South America—is the sweetest fruit in the family and the one with fewer seeds, which explains why it is so much appreciated. It is consumed fresh, as well as in the form of ice creams and other desserts.

Passion fruit (*Passiflora edulis*), also called *maracuyá* (from the Quechua word *murukuya*), is a climbing herb native to Brazil. Its name refers to the Passion of Christ, because, for pious Christians, the style of the flower was similar to the nails with which Jesus was crucified, while the five petals surrounded by a reddish crown stood for the five wounds of Jesus and the crown of thorns that was put on his head. What is actually eaten from the fruit are the seed kernels and the mucilage surrounding them, which are wrapped in a thin white coating that is just below the fruit's skin. One variety—*Passiflora ligularis*—mainly grows in the temperate highlands of the South American continent, and is commonly known as *parchita amarilla* or *parchita coloniera* in Venezuela, and as *granadilla* in Colombia.

Guava (*Psidium guajava*) is one of the 2,750 species of the *Myrtaceae* family. It is the fruit of a relatively tall tree with a fine smooth trunk, easily removable bark, grayish green rounded leaves, white flowers (not very big, but very beautiful), and round or pear-shaped fruits of four to eight centimeters (two to three inches) in diameter. The fruit has many small seeds surrounded by a sweet-sour generally reddish pulp that gives off a strong perfume when the fruit is ripe. This perfume may have led the great Linnaeus to name it *Psidium guajava*, as the Psidia region (a former Roman province of Asia Minor) was famous for producing the best perfumes of that time. Its Taino name, *guayaba*, was the word used to refer to this fruit from early on.

This beautiful and delicious fruit has been given special consideration by the food industry. There are many varied guava products in the market, among them guava nectar, marmalade, compote, or even frozen pulp.

Prickly pears (*Opuntia* spp.) are native to Mexico and the southwestern United States. In Latin America, this fruit is known as *tuna* and the cactus in which it grows as *nopal* (*Opuntia ficus indica*). This cactus is very versatile and propagates very easily, because its stalks grow on any land in which they are sown. Prickly pears were eaten by the Indians as they expanded throughout the whole continent. Today, the *Opuntia* species can be found almost everywhere in the world, except for the polar regions.

Cacao (*Theobroma cacao*) was called by Linnaeus *Theobroma* (food of the gods) due to the impression both the fruit and its history had made on him. Records of the origins of one of the most distinguished cacao varieties have been found in Venezuela. In fact, some experts have even argued that cacao is native to the region south of Lake Maracaibo, from where it then spread to the north and also to the west; others say that the plant is native to the Amazonian region. By contrast, the use of cacao as a beverage was an invention of the Central American pre-Hispanic tribes, who passed on this already ancient custom to the conquerors arriving from Europe. Clear evidence of this is the often described scene of the Aztec chief Montezuma offering conquistador Hernán Cortés the famous beverage.

Cacao-farming techniques have remained essentially the same up until the present. A visit to one of the farms would certainly show that all the practices carried out there—from sowing to harvesting—have been the same since very distant times. The tools are old, the facilities for drying and fermentation are centuries old, and the nomenclature used to refer to the various processes is ancient. One can say that this type of agricultural land use has survived since colonial times. Some progress has obviously taken place, especially in the fields of plant pathology and genetics, and there has been great progress in chocolate production.

The Europeans first used Indian labor to process cacao, but they were very soon replaced by slaves. Cacao and people of color have been thus related since the early colonial South American history.

Brought from Abroad

The coconut palm—baptized by Linnaeus as *Cocos nucifera*—is a member of the *Palmaceae* family, which includes 1,200 species that are spread throughout the world. It is native to Malaysia and the Pacific, from where it spread to the New World. This migration was not humankind's doing, though, but was rather the result of a fortuitous expansion that may have occurred by the ocean long before the fifteenth century, according to the experts. In his famous *Diccionario Crítico Etimológico* (Critical Etymological Dictionary), Corominas explains that the name *coco* was given to the fruit by Portuguese explorer Vasco da Gama's men in 1498, when they came across it in their voyage in the Asian seas. When the European sail-

Opening coconuts for milk, Sunday market, São Paulo, Brazil. © TRIP/
M. Barlow.

ors arrived in the Americas, coconuts already existed there, though only
in the southern part of the Central American isthmus. The discovery of
this elegant and fruitful palm in the New World gave rise to a great deal
of controversy on its origin, which has now been settled by demonstrating
that it is definitively native to Asia.

This big tropical nut is used for culinary purposes in a great variety of
ways, resulting in a number of delicious sweet and savory dishes, among
which the most remarkable are especially those that make up the South
American confectionery repertoire.

Bom—Bocado de Coco (Coconut Delight Dessert) (Bahia, Brazil)

- 4 cups water
- 1 pound sugar
- 8 eggs
- 1/4 pound butter
- 1/5 to 1/4 pound coconut, grated
- 1/4 pound wheat flour

Mix sugar and water until a syrup is made, caramelizing this mixture over low heat. Add the butter while cooking. Mix the eggs in a deep bowl without beating them. Add the syrup, grated coconut, and wheat flour, and mix well. Pour the mixture into previously greased or syrup-coated individual baking tins and oven-bake at moderate temperature until brown. (8 to 10 servings)

Bananas (*Musa paradisiaca*)—though native to Asia—were transferred by the Europeans to mainland Africa on the eve of the European contact in the Americas. They had then been brought to the Canary Islands and were transferred to Hispaniola in 1516 by Brother Tomás de Berlanga. This member of the *Musaceae* family not only grew well in the Caribbean Basin region, it also spread rapidly to the rain forest and even to the Andean zones. Plantains, which reproduce without the intervention of humankind, soon became a precious source of food for the Indians, Africans, and Europeans inhabiting the continent, often replacing wheat bread. This fruit contributes high nutritional values to the South American diet and is commonly eaten in different forms: roasted, boiled, or fried.

Tostones (Venezuela)

- 2 unripe plantains
- 1 cup vegetable oil
- salt to taste

Peel the plantains. Cut them into thin round slices. Fry the slices of plantain until they start to brown. Remove them from oil and let drain. Place them on a chopping board and flatten them with a mallet until their edges start to break. Fry them again until brown. Sprinkle with salt and serve on a platter.

Mangoes (*Mangifera indica*) are native to India. Mentioned in the Sanskrit texts of very ancient times, this tree was introduced to eastern Africa by the Arabs and then brought to the western side of the continent by the Portuguese, who eventually transplanted it in the eighteenth century to their colonies in northern Brazil, from where it spread in the second half of that century to the Antilles, the Guianas, and then to Venezuela. The fruit is eaten fresh, as well as in shakes and juices. It is also cooked to make up a sweet dish with syrup or made into jelly, the latter requiring that the fruit be unripe, which is then sweetened with cane sugar. Some time ago, people started to consume this fruit in the form of a chutney (a sort of marmalade), which has gained popularity up to the present.

Other important foreign fruits are oranges, mandarins, lemons, and pomelos. Botanists created the term *Rutaceae* to designate the family of plants, which includes rue and citrus, although some use the generic term *Aurantiaceae* to refer to the family of the latter, based on the yellow or golden color of their skins. According to paleobotanists, this family is about 20 million years old, thus having a great number of ancestors. These balloon-shaped fruits, say the economists, are among the five most important fruit products of the world, while, according to gastronomes, there is no doubt that they are among the most delicious ones. The members of this large family are native to Asia, from where the successive human migration waves brought about their expansion to Africa, Europe, and the Americas, mostly in ancient times. The most common of these fruits are sweet oranges (*Citrus sinensis* L.); bitter oranges (*Citrus aurantium* L.), also called in Spanish *naranja cajera*, *naranja de Sevilla*, or *bergamota*; green lemons (*Citrus aurantifolia* Christ.); mandarins (*Citrus reticulata* Blanco); pomelos (*Citrus maxima* Burm.); and citrons (*Citrus medica* L.). They are all very well known in South America, especially for their different uses at home—from juices to conserves and marmalades, to which they contribute their unique bitter taste.

Generally associated with breakfast and famous for their vitamin C content, oranges give their particular acidic taste and aroma to both desserts and main dishes. Moreover, thin strips of their crystallized skins constitute a much-beloved delicacy. A great proportion of their production is used by the food industry to make concentrates, juices, and marmalades.

Lemons, which have almost always been used on fish dishes, are also essential to the preparation of a number of South American fruit drinks. The most famous is the *agua de panela* or *papelón con limón* (an unrefined sugar, water, and lemon drink), which helped Venezuelans and Colombians resist the inclemency of the weather before carbonated beverages came into existence—the latter being mortal enemies of an ancient tradition.

Mandarins are not only sought after because of their unique sweet-sour taste, but also for the ease with which their skins peel and their segments come apart. They are also used to prepare refreshing juices, shakes, and sherbets. Although they grow well during the whole year, it is particularly in November and December when these deep-orange-colored balls proliferate in fruit stores and in stands along the streets, as well as in the markets, attracting everyone's attention with their vivid color that delights the senses.

Pomelos are usually consumed as juice, although sometimes they are eaten fresh at breakfast, by cutting them in two, removing the seeds, separating the segments with a special curved blade knife, and finally sprinkling sugar on top. They also are used in desserts, the most famous dishes being the *dulce de toronja en almíbar* (pomelos in sweet syrup) and *manjar* (prepared with the rose pomelo variety), the latter dish getting the first prize within the framework of the pomelo culinary repertoire.

All these citrus fruits except mandarins, which may have been introduced in the twentieth century, are recorded in the old South American documents of the sixteenth century, so they have taken on gastronomical significance in the countries of South America.

Grains Brought from Abroad and a Native Pseudocereal

Wheat

When the Europeans arrived in the Western Hemisphere, they were quite surprised to find a very large healthy and robust population who did not know wheat (*Triticum* spp.) and nourished themselves instead with cassava and corn. This was not easy to believe, as the words *wheat* and *sustenance* were synonyms to the inhabitants of the Old World.

When Europeans arrived in South America, they obviously tried to reproduce in the new lands their culinary traditions, in which wheat played a key role. They were not as successful everywhere as they had expected. The new seed mainly prospered in the areas with a mild climate, and, even there, Europeans faced the difficulties posed by the New World's voracious plagues affecting the crops. Nevertheless, they persevered to such an extent that they managed to acclimatize wheat not only to some parts of the Andes, but also in the Argentinean cultivable lands, where this grain is nowadays still produced in large quantities.

Because wheat was brought by the conquerors who ended up dominating the whole region, it was eventually considered to be superior to the remaining grains, and since the Iberian food culture spread throughout the whole continent, wheat has played a key role as an important ingredient in South American cuisine until current times.

Wheat flour is mainly used to make bread, of which there are different types depending on the South American country. It also plays a key role in the production of pasta—a food that has become a very important ingredient of the current regional diet, not only due to its low price, but also because it is easy to prepare. Wheat flour is also used to make different pastries and desserts. Although in some of the countries it has to be imported, wheat has become a basic product.

By the year 2001, the annual per-capita wheat consumption in South America amounted to 58.2 kilograms—more than twice the consumption of the South American native grain of choice, corn.

Rice

This grain (*Oryza sativa*) was brought to South America by the conquerors in the sixteenth century. There is proof that it was grown in Venezuela and Colombia at that time. Soon afterward, it was introduced in Peru, specifically in the Andean mountain range's east slope and in the Amazonian region. By the seventeenth century, it was grown in Brazil and in the other countries more to the south. During the second half of the eighteenth century, rice was extensively produced in the Guianas, which was very much related to the incorporation of land workers brought from India, Java, and China. Today, it is popular in South America, because of its low price and the fact that it can be easily obtained and is abundantly cultivated. In 2001 13,225 metric tons of rice were produced in South America, whereas 6,513 were produced in the United States. As for the consumption statistics, the annual per-capita rate is 29.9 kilograms, while that of the United States is only 9.2 kilograms.

Even though rice has been accepted in the South American gastronomy, it is only used as an accompaniment, as there are still objections to it being considered a main dish, probably due to its low nutritional value. But those holding such an opinion are perhaps unaware of the key role it plays as a main dish in many cuisines. In South America, an example is the Peruvian *arroz con pato*.

Quinoa

This dicotyledon (*Chenopodium quinoa*), whose seeds' albumens are rich in flour, has been classed as a pseudocereal. Its common name is from the Quechua language. It is native to South America and has been used since time immemorial by the Indians, who considered it the second most important grain, after corn. It was a holy plant for the Incas, who used it to pay tributes. Quinoa is resistant to unfavorable ground or climate conditions. It was extensively grown in the Andean region during pre-Columbian and even colonial times, becoming less important in republican times (i.e., in the nineteenth century), as it was replaced by other products such as corn. Today, quinoa is again gaining some ground thanks to the announcements made by the experts regarding its high nutritional value. Its cultivation is being developed again, which has resulted in a considerable increase in its consumption. This pseudocereal has been used in modern times in different ways—there is even a quinoa-based dish very similar to risotto. Today, flour obtained from dry quinoa kernels is sold in the market.

Herbs

Brought from Abroad

Parsley (*Petroselinum crispum* Mill.) was very well known in ancient times, though not as a flavoring agent, but as a medicine. Native to Macedonia and Central Asia, it was introduced in the South American continent by the European conquerors in the sixteenth century. The leaves of this herb are of a deep green color. There is a variety with densely curled leaves, which is known as curly parsley—in Spanish called *criolla*—and there is another variety with flat leaves called French or Spanish parsley. Parsley is consumed either raw or cooked, and it is one of the various herbs that serve as flavoring agents of broths and soups.

Coriander (*Coriandrum sativum*; in Spanish, *cilantro*) is native to the Old World. Its aroma and taste would bring back any South American to his or her childhood memories. Coriander is in fact an ingredient of all the cuisines of this region, to a lesser or greater extent, as it appears in many of the South American culinary preparations. It is used, for example, to prepare *pisca*—a kind of soup commonly consumed in the Venezuelan Andean region. Of all South Americans, those who are probably mostly keen on the use of coriander are Chileans, whose cuisine even features a sauce that is exclusively prepared with coriander, and a beverage on which it is based called *chinchivi*, which dates back to the late eighteenth century. This shows that Chileans have not paid much attention to the old popular Hispanic saying that goes "Coriander, good herb ... but not in excess."[2] When the conquerors arrived in South America, they found an herb with aroma and taste that were very similar to those of coriander, which they called *cilantro de monte* (wild coriander) or *culantro*. This is the *Eryngium foetidum*, which is botanically different from coriander, although naturalists included it in the same family—the *Umbelliferae*. Its leaves are a bit broader, elongated, and serrate-dentate. This herb is used as a substitute for coriander, especially in rural areas, and is not the only native herb used in South America, as demonstrated below.

Native

A great variety of herbs native to South America are used in the region. Only those that usually appear in the cookbooks representing the typical cuisines will be presented and described here.

Huacatay (*Tagetes minuta*) is a cultivated herb that grows wild in the coasts and mountains of Peru and in Amazonia. Its leaves and tender young shoots are used as condiment in the preparation of stews, roasts, and of one of the typical Peruvian dishes: the *pachamanca*.

Guasca (*Galinsoga parviflora* L.) is an herb from the *Compositae* family that has been used for culinary purposes by the South American Indians since ancient times. It is native to the Andean region of Colombia, and there it is mainly used as a condiment, although its use has also spread to other countries. *Guasca* is essential for a soup prepared in Bogotá known as *ajiaco*.

Jambú (*Spilanthes acmella* Murr. and *Spilanthes oleracea* L.) is an herb native to tropical Brazil. In English it is called "paracress," while in Portuguese it is either called *agrião do Brasil*, *agrião do Pará*, or *jambú*. It is used for the preparation of some typical dishes of the Amazonian region, like *Pato no tucupí* and *tacacá*, which is a thick soup flavored with *tucupí* (cooked juice from bitter cassava), dry shrimp, sometimes freshwater fish, and the *jambú*. The leaves have a slightly numbing effect on the tongue and the mouth because of their hot flavor, compared by some people to that of pepper.

Meat

Beef

The first South American cities started to emerge as soon as the conquerors' settlements transformed from camps into villages. These new population centers would start from the main plaza square, the streets always following the city-planning grid pattern inherited from ancient Rome. The Cabildo was established as the main authority to regulate the different activities in the new societies, one of the most important being wares supply. Beef provision and trade was particularly important, as the Europeans could not do without it, and the Indians who had undergone transculturation also demanded it to a certain extent. Meat supply was carried out by means of a sort of tender—called *remate* in the old texts—that had to be attended by those who owned cattle and had any interest in selling them. On a sheet of paper, they had to specify the price of an *arroba* of beef (about 30 pounds) and that of the other cattle products such as suet. They also had to state the way they would charge the money, either cash or by means of land-products bartering, because in the sixteenth and seventeenth centuries, cash was considerably scarce.

The tender winner would be granted written permission to sell meat to the neighbors for a year. This person could proceed "to weigh the beef joints," as it was referred to at that time and even in more recent times. This is precisely where the Spanish expression *pesa* (weighing) comes from, used in the past to refer to the butcher's shop and remembered by many people from their childhood—a name that has changed, though, into *frigorífico* (fridge) as a result of the modernization of the process to preserve this food.

Beef became the food of choice for the South American town and city dwellers, playing a role in the repertoire of typical dishes, the *asado argentino* (Argentinean roast) being perhaps the most famous. Traditionally, beef has to be very well done in South America in order to be eaten, in contrast to the American barbecue, which is rather eaten rare. This habit dates back to the early regional history of farming, as cattle were mainly used in colonial times as a source of leather, which was a very important export good. After cattle processing, lots of meat was left over, and since the modern food preserving methods of refrigeration did not yet exist, meat had to be cut into strips—*tasajo* or *cecina*—and then salted. These pieces of meat had to be desalted before consumption, and usually they were then boiled (if a soup was to be prepared), fried, or cooked. Frying or cooking required grinding or shredding. In these most common culinary preparations beef was neither juicy nor reddish, as is the case of fresh grilled or fried beef. This tradition took root to such an extent that even today, when Uruguayans or Argentineans prepare their *asado* (roast), they like it well done. The same is true for the *bistec criollo* typical of Venezuela and Colombia, which is a thin beefsteak that needs to cook for a long time. Jerky (dry salted meat) is used in Bolivia to prepare a typical dish known as *majao*.

Majao (Bolivia)

- 3/4 pound jerky
- 10 cups water
- 4 tablespoons oil
- 2 cups rice
- 5 eggs
- 5 medium slices ripe plantain or cassava
- 2 medium onions, peeled and finely chopped
- 1/2 tomato, chopped and seeded

- 1/4 paprika, chopped and seeded
- 1/2 teaspoon salt
- 1/2 teaspoon pepper
- 1 teaspoon ground oregano

Sofrito. Pour three tablespoons of oil in a frying pan. When it is very hot, add the onions, tomatoes, paprika, oregano, salt, and pepper. Sauté for about 15 minutes. Set aside.

Dish. Cook jerky in 4 cups of water for 1/2 hour or until just right for eating. Let it cool. Then, remove from water, place on a chopping board, and crush slightly using the blade of the kitchen knife. Shred into thin strips. Add the shredded meat to the *sofrito*. If the mixture is dry, add some of the cooking stock.

Brown the rice in a separate frying pan with the remaining tablespoon of oil. Set the remaining 6 cups of water to a boil; add the browned rice, jerky, and *sofrito* mixture. Stir well. Cook over high heat for 10 minutes, and then over low heat for 5 minutes, making sure that it does not dry out. Serve with a fried egg and a piece of fried plantain or fried cassava. (5 servings)

One of the peculiarities of beef sale in South America is the great variety of names used to refer to the cuts of meat, which are not only different from those of Europe and the United States, but also among themselves in the region, varying from one country to another both in shape and name. This could be referred to as a real gastronomic Babel, hindering communication between people from different countries. The following are some clarifying examples of the different names given to some meat cuts that can be considered to be almost homologous. The beef rib section would correspond more or less to what is known in Argentina as the *bife ancho*, which, in turn, is in some way equivalent to the Venezuelan *solomo de cuerito*. The sirloin cut, to give another example, would correspond to the Argentinean *lomo*, which is known in Venezuela as *lomito*. What is referred to as *tira de asado* in the south is known as *costilla* in the north, and what is called *cuadril* in the former is *punta trasera* in the latter, and so on and so forth depending on the country.

Pork

In colonial times, South Americans used to eat the Iberian pork species, but, with time, a wide range of varieties started to be consumed, as new species were imported both from Europe and North America. The South American cuisine features many culinary preparations that use loin with bones in the form of steaks, as well as ham, which is still prepared at home following the traditional recipes like that of the so-called *jamón del país* from Peru. Chops are used in the typical stews and in Chinese dishes. Pork legs are famous in the whole continent. Pork fat and bacon are obviously consumed too, the latter now industrially produced. The countless and varied farmhouse or industrially produced sausages deserve a chapter to themselves, ranging from blood sausages, chorizos, and spicy sausages of Spanish-Portuguese origin to the German-style sausages introduced by the successive migration waves of Germans.

Goat

Unlike porcine meat, caprine meat—also very popular in the continent—has not undergone an industrialization process, which explains why it is still prepared in very traditional ways, generally only at home and in certain typical restaurants. Cheese is the only goat product that is produced on a certain industrial scale, though it is only consumed in some places and, more recently, in big cities, where it is sold as a delicacy. Sweets can also be made from goat milk.

Lamb

One of the domestic animals that goes a long way back is sheep (*Ovis aries*). By the time of the discovery and conquest of the Americas there were many herds in the Iberian Peninsula. It was only to be expected that the European conquerors would load these animals on their ships, and that, once settled in the new lands, these would multiply and be adopted by the natives. There have always been two very good reasons to raise this animal: its wool and its meat. As it met the clothing and food demands of the peoples, sheep soon became very popular at that time. Besides, lamb consumption in South America has been reinforced by the Iberian, French, Italian, Arab, and Hebrew traditions since the late nineteenth century, both at home and in restaurants, to the extent that nowadays one can say that lamb is consumed more frequently than in the past.

The Llama Family

The consumption of South American *camelidae* has been considerably reduced until the present, still taking place in rural areas of countries such as Ecuador, Peru, and Bolivia. It is not commonly found in cities—only sometimes in certain typical restaurants, as is the case of Peru, where there is a traditional meal known as *olluquito con charqui* (*charqui* being salted llama meat). There is no doubt that this drop in consumption has been the result of new legislation and a number of protectionist measures, as well as of the abundance of other meat types in the market.

Poultry: Chicken, Turkey, and Duck

The domestic birds that soon adapted to the New World, and whose breeding spread throughout it, are nowadays industrially bred, so it is difficult to find examples of domestic corn-fed breeding, as it was done in the past. This means that a parallel industry has emerged aimed at producing food for poultry farms. Today, because chicken and hen meat is plentiful, most people can afford to buy it, and it has been progressively replacing beef, especially among the lower classes.

Most turkeys produced in South America are either bred in medium or large poultry farms or imported from the United States. Turkey has gained popularity in South America, due to the influence of the American customs. It is essentially prepared for Christmas, combined with the other typical national dishes, such as the *hallaca*—the Venezuelan Christmas tamale.

Ducks are less popular, though they are still important, for example in Peru and Brazil. Chinese immigration has been fostering the consumption of these web-footed birds recently, as many Asian dishes feature their meat. All Chinese restaurants have a duck-based dish on their menu.

Eggs

Hen eggs were incorporated in the South American diet with the arrival of the Europeans early in the sixteenth century. This food is consumed in its raw form or cooked as an independent dish at any time of the day, but it is also an ingredient of countless savory and sweet dishes. By mixing eggs with olive oil and seasoning them with garlic, salt, and vinegar, one obtains the most important and delicious sauce of the Spanish-Portuguese tradition: mayonnaise. In the past, its preparation required a lot of patience, a strong arm for whipping, a special knack in the wrist, and the slow incorporation of fat into the mixture in order to be successful. Today, electrical appliances have reduced the time needed and the risks of failing when preparing mayonnaise.

Game

The lowland tapir (*danta*) is mainly found in South American forested areas. This mammal is almost as large as a horse, but it is particularly heavy and stout. It has a trunk that is simply a large movable nose. Under the threat of being hunted, lowland tapirs can react violently, lowering their heads and using all their heftiness to knock down their opponent head-on. This is the reason why they were never easy prey for the Indians, who lacked firearms. They love rivers, where they go to bathe and where they swim easily. Lowland tapirs are usually active at night. Their meat was eaten by the indigenous peoples and soon caught the attention of the Europeans. The first stories heard in the Old World about lowland tapirs were announced by the chronicler Peter Martyr d'Anghiera in his famous *Décadas oceánicas* (Ocean Decades).

The stories told by the travelers of the nineteenth and twentieth century often recorded the consumption of *danta* meat—either grilled fresh, or salted, desalted, and then shredded and fried in lard or oil, the latter dish known as *pisillo* in the Venezuelan and Colombian plains as well as in the Guianas. Nowadays, there are protection laws in all South American countries against the indiscriminate hunting of lowland tapirs.

The peccary—known in the region as *báquiro, tallasú,* or *pecari*—can be described as a sort of American wild boar, which is less hefty than the European strain and does not have a tail. Classed by zoologists as members of the *Tayassuidae* family, peccaries have a dorsal gland that the conquest chroniclers thought was their navel. Through this fleshy bump these animals release a strong, musky odor. However, their meat was very much appreciated by the Indians, then by the Europeans and thus by the *criollos*. Peccaries live in herds, and when they feel threatened they ferociously charge their enemy as a group. They can be very dangerous toward imprudent people who dare confront them; the most advisable thing to do is to climb a tree or a high rock. This animal is sought after both for its skin and for its tasty meat. However, peccary hunting has also been very much regulated by protectionist laws.

The paca or *lapa* is a rodent that resembles a South American hare. Classed by the specialists as a member of the *Caviidae* family, pacas were considered to be precious game by Indians and then by the European conquerors and colonists. They have been hunted until the present and are now in danger of extinction in some places; therefore, they are also protected by laws banning paca hunting or only allowing it during a short season. Their meat has been compared to that of piglets, as pacas have a lot of fat, although the taste is much stronger.

Capybaras (*chigüire, capibara,* or *carpincho*) are referred to scientifically as *Hydrochaerus hydrochaeris*, which means "aquatic-terrestrial, aquatic-terrestrial," stressing the capybaras' amphibious habits. They are the world's largest rodents and have short legs to sustain their voluminous bodies, no tail, a big head with small ears, and coarse fur. The fatty meat of this sort of "water pig"—as it was once called by some chroniclers—is very much sought after and particularly appreciated by the Venezuelan and Columbian *llaneros*. It is eaten either fresh or salted and then prepared in the aforementioned *pisillo* form. Along with iguanas, armadillos, and terrapins, capybaras are commonly hunted during Lent, as the Catholic Church did not forbid the consumption of their meat during this time of the year based on their amphibious habits.

Armadillos—from the *Dasipodidae* family—are probably the typical South American edentate animals. There are many different species of armadillo in South America, but the smaller ones are mostly consumed. They are scarce and only eaten in rural areas, due to the existing protectionist policies and the difficulties involved in hunting this animal. However, there are some typical armadillo-based dishes in South America. For example, in Brazil (in the region of Minhas Gerais), a dish called *Tutu de feijão à mineira* is prepared using armadillo meat.

As for venison, the South American members of the *Cervidae* family are represented by a number of genera. There is the Andean deer or *huemules*, living in the southern end of the Argentinean and Chilean mountain range; the marsh deer—known as *veado galheiro grande* in Brazil—which is higher than the Andean race; the pampas deer (*ciervo de las Pampas*), known in Argentina as *venado* and in Brazil as *veado campeiro*; and others from the *Mazama* genus, which are smaller than the others mentioned, but very much appreciated, especially in Venezuela and Colombia. Venison is considerably sought after and represents an important prey for those who devote themselves to this sport, which is incidentally also regulated through a great number of legal policies aimed at protecting the species.

Viscacha—a member of the *Chinchillidae* family—is a rodent that mainly abounds in Peru and Argentina and can be found either on the plains and the mountains. Its meat is white and very tasty, which explains why is it hunted and consumed quite regularly in the country without much culinary elaboration. In modern times, farms have been established for the raising of this hare-like animal, which is now also canned in pickling brine and sold in Argentinean supermarkets, transforming viscacha into somewhat of a mass consumption product.

The *ñandú* or South American ostrich (*Rhea americana*) is typically found in the southern part of the continent, northeastern Brazil, and eastern Bolivia. This animal has been hunted since pre-Hispanic times with implements invented by the South American Indians called *boleadoras avestruceras* (ostrich bolas). These consisted of two balls made of stone (or any other heavy material) covered with leather and strongly tied with thongs. The hunter would wield the *boleadora* by one of the balls—called the *manija* (handle)—powerfully whirl the other ball above his head, and subsequently throw the weapon to entangle the neck of the ostrich, which would fall to the ground as a result. With the arrival of the Europeans, a third ball was incorporated to the *boleadoras*, in order to use them to catch cattle by throwing them to their legs. Today, *ñandúes* are raised in farms, as their meat has become a valuable product that is considered a rarity, and which is served more and more often in restaurants. In Uruguay, *ñandú* raising has proliferated, becoming an interesting export item.

Nuts

There are a great variety of nuts, among which the most famous in South America are walnuts (*Juglans* spp.), almonds (*Prunus amygdalon*), hazelnuts (*Corylus* spp.), macadamias (*Macadamia integrifolia*), pecans (*Carya* spp.), Brazil nuts (*Bertholettia excelsa*), and cashews (*Anacardium occidentale*). Pecans, cashews, and Brazil nuts are native to the American continent, the latter two specifically to South America, present in the Guianas and the Amazonian region for time immemorial.

Peanuts (*Arachis hypogaea*) are the fruits of a leguminous plant native to the South American continent, which may have originated in Brazil or Bolivia. However, *peanut* is a Taino word, thus of West Indian origin. They are not only consumed as fruits per se, but are also used in the manufacture of vegetable oils, as well as sauces and sweets, especially nougats. Due to their great nutritional value, their consumption is also widely recommended.

Onions

The *Liliaceae* family stands out in botanic repertoires for having many members, but also because more than a few species play a key role in a great number of typical dishes of the region. The onion—*Allium cepa*, for the naturalists—is a basic ingredient common to all South American stews that, despite its humble nature, has been essential in the whole continent, for both poor and rich. They all have been delighted in this vegetable, which—as Chilean poet Pablo Neruda once said in his famous "Ode to the Onion"—makes people cry without hurting them. The onion arrived in South America very early, in conquerors' and missionaries' knapsacks, and was grown with success levels that have been maintained until the present.

Another bulb from the same family is the chive (*Allium schoenoprasum* L.). Known as *cebollín, cebollino,* or *cebollina* in Spanish and corresponding to the famous French *ciboulette,* chives are extensively harvested and consumed in South America.

Garlic

If the onion is the lady of the *Amaryllidaceae,* garlic has to be considered the gentleman, due to its fundamental role. After a long but productive journey from Central Asia to the New World, this member of the family, called *Allium sativum* by botanists, was brought by the Europeans and settled itself in the South American subsoil and cauldrons. In Spanish, garlic bulbs are called *cabezas de ajo* (garlic heads) and their pieces or cloves are known as *dientes de ajo* (garlic teeth). This rhizome can be white, reddish, or purplish depending on the variety. The unmistakable flavor it gives to food is so strong and peppery that it makes people use it in moderation, but at the same time it is so much associated with the traditional taste preferences of the peoples of the region that it would simply be impossible not to use it. Cold weather and dryness favor its cultivation. The bigger the size of its cloves (which depends on the garlic variety), the smoother its flavor.

Spices

In Spanish, the spices used for cooking are called *especias,* which is different from the word *especie,* which means class, category, or group of equal elements. Before the arrival of the Europeans in the New World, the indigenous populations knew of and used some spices, which then won well-deserved fame throughout the whole world. Hot pepper (*Capsicum* spp.)—called "the pepper from the Indies" by the Europeans—and vanilla (*Vanilla planifolia*), which both disconcerted and captivated the conquerors, are only two examples of what can be called "the new spices" within the historical framework of the Western culture. These two spices play a very important role in South American cuisine.

Pepper

The common spices known as black or white pepper (*Piper nigrum*) are members of the *Piperaceae* family, a term that derives from the Sanskrit word *pippali*, alluding to the fact that this plant is native to the Malabar Island and southern India. It is currently grown in the tropical regions around the globe.

Except for some isolated (though successful) cases, the attempts to introduce pepper in the Spanish American lands from the sixteenth to the eighteenth century failed. It was not until the nineteenth century that it began to be cultivated both in the Antilles (Santo Domingo, Trinidad, and Puerto Rico) and in South America, showing considerable success in French Guiana, from where it was then brought more to the south, to the Pará River region (Brazil), late in that century.

Cinnamon

The fact that cinnamon is a bark is what makes it so particular among spices from a botanical point of view. This originality is obviously reinforced by its penetrating aroma and pungent taste. One of the justifications Columbus put forward in order to get backing for his risky voyage to the New World was the offer to bring cinnamon to Spain without having to go through the long, complicated, and expensive trading circuit people had to cover by land and then through the Mediterranean in order to gain access to this precious ingredient.

During colonial times, the Spanish tried to introduce cinnamon in South America, but they were frustrated in their attempts, as they did not manage to cultivate a single plantation, and the trees of the species they transplanted ended up as a garden curiosity. However, they found out that there was a plant with a bark that had a similar aroma to that of authentic cinnamon. This plant was *Aniba canelilla*, known in Venezuela as *canelilla*, in Brazil as *casca do maranhão*, in Peru as *canela muena*, and in Colombia as *canela de Santa Fe*. It was used as a medicine to fight arthritis, chronic colds, and other illnesses. In the eighteenth century, the Colombian sage Celestino Mutis, who carried out a famous botanic exploration focused on useful plants, promoted the use of this cinnamon variety as a substitute for the original one, following the then common trend of finding aromatic products in the Spanish America that could replace the Asiatic ones. This South American cinnamon is still used in rural areas. In general terms, cinnamon is used both in the form of sticks, to scent certain desserts during their preparation, and ground, sprinkling it over custards and other sweet dishes.

Cloves

Among the numerous members of the *Myrtaceae* family, the *Eugenia caryophyllata* Thunb. stands out for its prominent organoleptic (sensory) characteristics. This is the plant that produces the worldwide famous clove—in Spanish called *clavo de especia* or *clavo de olor*—which the Spaniards are said to have called *garofe* in the seventeenth century, and which, even in the following century, can be found as *girophle* in the *Diccionario de Autoridades* (Spain's dictionary of attributed quotations). It is native to the Moluccas Archipelago, but this fact was zealously concealed as a secret by the Oriental peoples, and later on by the Portuguese and Spanish seafarers, who even forged the charts once they had arrived in the islands in the sixteenth century in order to conceal the approach routes leading to the place where this aromatic plant used to grow, as its trading price was very high at that time.

During the eighteenth century, a number of attempts were made to transplant cloves to the Guianas, Brazil, Jamaica, Martinique, Haiti, and even Trinidad, with no remarkable success. This spice did not prosper in the Americas, but in the countries where its trade flourished, it became an imported good from the very early colonial times, and its demand has not decreased since. It played a remarkable role in Spanish cuisine and began to be used in South America when the conquerors arrived. This spice took root in a great number of dishes that are nowadays an integral part of the regional culinary heritage, especially that of sweet dishes.

Cumin

This member of the *Umbelliferae* family—called *Cuminum cyminum* by Linnaeus—is a small annual herb of white or rose flowers, with tiny and very aromatic fruits, whose seeds have played a role in the human diet for as long as memory can recall. South Americans use cumin seeds often, as a result of the Spanish and Portuguese influence. They use it so much that those who are not accustomed to the flavor usually find it repulsive.

Aniseed

This beautiful member of the *Ubelliferae* family was baptized by Linnaeus as *Pimpinella anisum*—a compound name of a hybrid nature, as the first term derives from the Latin word *bipennula* (having two wings) and the second term from the Greek word *anison* (which could be translated as "matchless"). This aromatic plant is said to have originated in Egypt. It was grown in South America since the early colonial times, as it adapted to the new lands with relative ease. Its seed is used both in baking and in the preparation of sweet dishes. It is impossible to forget mentioning star anise or "Chinese anise," also called *badiana*. This is the variety botanists designated as *Illicium verum* Hook., a name that alludes to its organoleptic characteristics, because it means "real seduction." The cultivation of this type of anise was not as successful as that of common anise, although it has prospered in some regions, like Ecuador.

Vanilla

Botanists called it *Vanilla planifolia*, alluding to its capsule-like elongated fruits and its flat leaves. This herbaceous plant is a member of the very large *Orchidaceae* family. According to some experts, it is native to Central America, where it was found by the Spanish in the early conquest times, surprising and delighting their sense of smell. Other specialists argue that it is native to the Amazonian region. In modern times, synthetic vanilla can be produced through the chemical processing of eugenol—obtained by distilling clove essence. This type of vanilla has gained more ground in the market due to its lower price, but it has not been able to replace the natural one within the framework of haute confectionery, because it lacks the unique aroma of the latter. Nevertheless, this synthetic vanilla essence is currently used in all South American countries.

Tomatoes

According to the Renaissance physician Francisco Hernández, in the Viceroyalty of New Spain (Mexico) there were numerous varieties of a fruit that had been designated by the Aztecs with different names, among them *tomatl* and *xitomatl*, from the Nahuatl language; later on it was baptized as *Lycopersicon esculentum* Mill. by the botanists, who considered it to be a member of the *Solanaceae* family and native to the New World. However, specialists are still debating whether this fruit originated in Central America or in the Andes. In the eighteenth century, a wild variety was found in Peru, commonly known as *tomate cimarrón*. South American natives ate it in its raw form as a fruit. The use of tomatoes as a condiment or as a base for the preparation of sauces emerged and was improved during Spanish domination.

Spaniards who went to the Americas familiarized themselves with the use of the tomato from the very beginning, but it took longer for

Outdoor Chilean market. © TRIP/J. Drew.

it to cross the borders of the Iberian Peninsula and spread throughout the rest of the European continent, as it had a reputation for being poisonous, just like many of its relatives from the *Solanaceae* family. After Spain, Italy is said to have been the first country that accepted tomatoes as part of their cuisine. Tomatoes were then incorporated in all European culinary repertoires, playing a very important role up until the present.

There are different varieties of this fruit, basically due to their differences in shape. The most important ones are the *tomate manzano*, which—as suggested by the Spanish name—is similar to an apple (*manzana*); the *tomate perita* (plum tomato), which is similar to a small pear (*perita*) or plum; and the small *tomate cereza* (cherry tomato), similar to the cherry (*cereza*). South American cuisines still feature the use of raw tomatoes in salads, but also of its cooked form as an ingredient of one of the key basic sauces of many of their typical dishes, namely the *sofrito*.

Vegetable Oils: Sesame, Peanut, Palm (*Dendé*), and Corn

Until recently, frying and pastry cooking were done with pork and beef lard, which explains why vegetable oil does not appear in the traditional cookbooks of the region. The only vegetable oil used since colonial times has been olive oil—called *aceite de Castilla* (oil from Castile) at that time—almost exclusively used in salads. It was not until the twentieth century that the use of vegetable oils obtained from corn, sesame, peanuts, sunflower seeds, and even soy became popular, as local industries were established. However, this change was also the result of the imports of vegetable oils, mostly from the United States. The introduction of this new type of fat resulted in a considerably lighter diet on the one hand and in a slight change in the taste of fried food and typical South American sweet dishes that traditionally used animal fat on the other. At the same time, vegetable fat started to be produced, especially for confectionery purposes. Although the use of animal fats has not totally disappeared from the South American cuisine, it is nowadays very limited, existing only in certain rural locales. The per-capita consumption of animal fats in 2001 amounted to 2.8 kilograms.

In the twentieth century, olive-oil imports also increased due to the immigration of Italians, Spaniards, and Portuguese, which boosted this product's demand and eventually popularized it throughout the whole South American region. However, olive-oil consumption has not increased significantly since then, the annual per-capita consumption not being higher than 0.1 kilograms. In Chile and Argentina the olive-oil sector is starting to develop.

NOTES

1. *The Visual Encyclopedia of Food* (New York: Macmillan, 1996), p. 345.
2. "Es bueno cilantro ... pero no tanto."

3

Cooking

WOMEN'S WORK

In each of the three cultures that played a role in the history of the South American society, cooking has always been considered women's work. South American women in charge of the domestic chores were the ones who developed a type of cuisine that mixed the traditions of Indians, Europeans, and Africans. This cuisine became known as *cocina criolla*.

South American Natives

Since pre-Columbian times there has been a clear gendered division of labor among Indians. Men are the leaders of the communities, perform the religious duties, are the specialists in rituals and cures (the so-called *chamanes*), and are in charge of constructing the houses and other buildings, as well as of fighting wars, hunting, fishing, and preparing the land for cultivation. The women's job is to carry out the culinary tasks, as well as those related to the sowing and harvesting of the primary food sources. This implies that women only leave their village or shantytown to do the farm work in the nearby field.

Perhaps the only exception to the rule stating that cooking is solely a woman's task is roasting meat—game meat in particular—which is performed by men in a primitive manner. They are in charge of lighting the bonfire and throwing the bagged animal in the fire or on the embers, often without previously skinning or plucking it. It is the *llaneros* and the gauchos who are actually in charge of roasts.

Women do not simply cook corn and cassava; they also prepare *casabe* or *mañoco*, as well as sauces based on the use of capsicum and some herbs. They also serve the prepared food to the men and do not partake in the act of eating with them—they would eat alone and at the end of the meal. A similar habit is common in many South American households. In fact, in both rural huts and humble urban houses, those who sit at the table to eat are the men—the head of the family and his older sons—while the woman serves them the dishes she has prepared, keeping some food for herself, which she eats at the end of the meal, often in the kitchen. Setting the table and washing the dishes have always been a woman's task.

Europeans

The conquerors' habits were somewhat similar, as they considered kitchen labor to be in the domain of women. As far as the housework is concerned—with the exception of the male cooks working for the court or for wealthy households—Europeans followed the same pattern of South American Indians. This habit, strongly related to the Arab traditions in which the woman had to stay confined in the house most of the time, is reflected in certain old sayings that are still on many people's lips, such as "Mujer honrada, en casa y pierna quebrada" (The honorable woman, at home with a broken leg); "El tocino hace la olla, el hombre, la plaza y la mujer, la casa" (The bacon in the pot, the men out in the world and the women at home); and "La olla y la mujer, reposadas han de ser" (Both pots and women should always be quiet).[1]

Africans

The role with African women has always been limited to the farming and cooking duties. As an exception, the men in charge of the religious worship perform the sacrifice and also prepare the propitiatory victims (often birds) during the liturgical ceremonies. As for the kitchen work, women have played a key role in the improvement of certain grinding, fermenting, and food-preservation practices, and have therefore been responsible for a relative progress in the field of cooking technique.

The Ever-Growing Number of Exceptions

There are exceptions to the traditional concept of cooking always being women's work. The evolution of this line of work until today shows the emergence of male culinary-related duties on a daily basis.

The Cooks of the Past

During colonial times there were certain exceptions to the rule that associated cooking with women. Various types of documents refer to male slave cooks who probably learned the trade in the New World, as they had no other option under the conquerors' domination. Slaves were considered to be objects—or at least machines—and were thus included in wills, in which the trade they mastered was sometimes also mentioned, as this implied a certain added value. There are also records of domestic servants in newspaper notices published by masters claiming slaves who had run away, and their characteristics were specified to facilitate their capture. Even though these individuals are sometimes described as skillful cooks, most of them probably did not master the trade, either because they had learned it by force or because of their usually low educational level. Most of them were illiterate and were engaging in the particular task for the first time in their lives. However, there were some exceptions to this rule, such as the famous cordon bleu of the Viceroyalty of the River Plate known as Monsieur Ramón ("Raymond" spelled in the Spanish way), who ran an academy in the late eighteenth century, where the slaves of wealthy households would go to learn how to cook.[2]

According to the chronicles of colonial times—especially from the eighteenth century—as well as of the subsequent republican times, there were also foreign cooks, almost always French or Italian, who worked for important officials or very wealthy families. Examples of this were viceroys and captains general. In the Viceroyalty of Santa Fe—now more or less Colombia and part of Venezuela—Viceroy Manuel de Guirior had a so-called Monsieur Lasala as a cook in 1773; there was also the cook of Santiago de Liniers (viceroy of the River Plate), the French Pierre Payette, in 1795. Another interesting piece of information about the presence of French cooks in the culinary field is available thanks to the descriptions made of the banquet held in honor of River Plate Viceroy Aviles on March 14, 1799, in nearby Buenos Aires—a dinner that went down in history, in which Joseph Dure is said to have been the main cook and Pierre Botet the pastry cook.[3] There are documents recording that, in 1799, François Combe and then Juan Bautista Botelle were the cooks of Manuel de Guevara Vasconcelos (captain general of Venezuela).[4] As for colonial Brazil, Gilberto Freyre confirms the European origin of the cooks, who made up a "cooking staff working for captains general or viceroys, noblemen from overseas and rich people, also of European origin, aristocratic expressions of a transoceanic aristocracy, though, that had no roots in the new lands."[5]

But also in republican times, the presidents of the emerging South American republics had French cooks working for them. To give one significant example, in 1826, the French cook Louis Lemoyiven and the pastry cook François Fremont were part of Simón Bolívar's entourage in Lima.[6]

The situation in Brazil was similar. When Portugal's King João VI left Lisbon, escaping from the invasion of Napoléon Bonaparte's troops, to settle the vast Brazilian colonies, he had French cooks taken to Rio de Janeiro, the new capital of the monarchy. After Brazil's independence was declared and King João's son, Pedro I, was proclaimed emperor, Gallic (male) cooks continued to be preferred, as they were during the lengthy reign of Pedro II. This Braganza family had to maintain a court that lived as luxuriously as possible; thus, the imperial kitchens had to be endowed with such human resources to ensure the good taste that befitted the magnificence of great state festivities at that time.

The practice of cooking by men was therefore associated with foreign ways and, in any case, these services could only be afforded by high dignitaries and other wealthy people.

During the second half of the nineteenth century and at least until the 1930s there were establishments, usually run by foreign ladies, devoted to training young women to be domestic servants and especially providing them with the culinary knowledge needed to be good servants. These were the first cooking academies exclusively for women, but they obviously paved the way for the modern cooking schools for both male and female students.

The New Culinary Vocations

During the nineteenth and the first half of the twentieth centuries, the continental panorama did not change significantly. However, in the second half of the twentieth century, the cooking profession flourished in Europe—particularly in France—and those practicing it gained considerable social prestige and a high economic status, which soon had an influence on South America. It was mainly during the 1970s that the expansion of mass communications and the consequent globalization phenomenon brought about the emergence of many culinary vocations—especially of men. Young men could explain to their parents that the culinary profession was neither only for women nor socially unacceptable at the international level. This is how the traditional conception of male cooks changed and an era of professionalization began, with the creation of cooking schools in the main South American cities. In Argentina, the following schools emerged: the Instituto de Gastronomía Profesional Mausi Sebess; the Instituto Argentino de Gastronomía; the International Buenos Aires Hotel and Restaurant School (IBAHRS); Ott College, Acassuso; the Bue Trainers; the CESYT—Centro de Estudios Sociales y Technológicos; the Escuela Argentina de Cocineritos; and the Escuela de Gastronomía of the Instituto Superior Mariano Moreno, all in Buenos Aires; Azafrán (a school for the training of professional cooks) and Celia Escuela Integral Gastronómica, both in Córdoba; and the Escuela de Cocineros Patagónicos, located in Patagonia.

In Peru: Le Cordon Bleu Peru, the Escuela de Alta Cocina D'Gallia, the Escuela de Cocina Chef Bleu, and the Escuela de Alta Cocina of the Instituto de los Andes, all located in Lima. In Brazil: the Atelier Gourmand and the Escola Wilma Kövesi de Cozinha, located in São Paulo. In Venezuela: the Centro de Estudios Gastronómicos (CEGA), the Instituto Culinario de Caracas, the Instituto Superior de Artes Culinarias, and the Centro Venezolano de Capacitación Gastronómica, all located in Caracas.

The emergence of cooking schools, fostered by the considerable increase especially in the number of young men showing serious interest in the culinary arts, changed the panorama that had prevailed for centuries in the continent. It paved the way both for the study of modern culinary techniques and for the need for innovation in the preparation of the typical South American dishes.

Today, prizes are awarded to young cooks in an attempt to emulate the great European cookery competitions, such as the Bocuse d'Or. This is the case of the Gran Concurso Culinario Latinoamericano Azteca, which was held for the first time, in Mexico City, in 2003. At the same time, associations of Latin American chefs have been created, like the Foro Panamericano de Asociaciones Culinarias Profesionales, the Asociación de Chefs del Perú (ACHEP), Los Amigos de los Chefs (in Quito, Ecuador), the Asociación de Chefs de Bolivia (in La Paz, Bolivia), the Associação Brasileira Da Alta Gastronomia (ABAGA, in São Paulo, Brazil), and the Asociación Uruguaya de Chefs (in Montevideo, Uruguay). The members of these professional associations are mostly young people who have been studying at the regional schools and also at foreign ones, such as the Culinary Institute of America or Le Cordon Bleu. They serve to foster their members' professional improvement, implement better working conditions, and act as employment agencies and contacts with foreign associations for exchange programs.

Today, hotels, restaurants, public institutions, private firms, and even wealthy families look to both cooking schools and professional associations to get skilled labor. Besides, the figure of the culinary entrepreneur has emerged in the past few years, resulting in the establishment of new restaurants, often holding the name of the founder chef and offering what could be designated as *cuisine d'auteur*.

COOKING STYLES

There are two coexisting cooking styles: a rural one, with the traditional procedures resulting in rustic but still delicious food, and an urban one, in which the resources of modern culinary technology are used and the aesthetic needs are taken into consideration for the creation of a product that better meets the contemporary visual and taste expectations.

Two Coexisting Worlds

As most of the population in contemporary South America live in cities, the accelerated urban development experienced in the continent during the second half of the twentieth century would seem to have brought about drastic changes in people's habits. However, this has not been exactly the case, as the rural population that migrated to the cities carried their food habits with them. Besides, the household structure has not undergone radical changes, so rural habits still persist in urban households, obviously mixed with some features of the modern age, but keeping up the old traditions to a greater extent. This phenomenon not only shows in family relationships, but especially within the culinary sphere.

The Rural World

A number of traditional elements can still be found in the different cooking processes, especially in the rural communities. These people still use coal or firewood stoves, clay containers, and ancient utensils such as the round iron griddle called a *budare* or *aripo* in Venezuela and a *callana* in Colombia, which is used to cook corn-based dishes. The old manual machines made of cast iron and used for grinding corn have not disappeared either. This is also true for the grinding stone or *metate* (also called a *batán*) and of the large wooden mortars called *pilones*, also used to grind corn, which have not fallen into disuse. The kneading of the typical corn breads is still done by hand, and when the typical sweet dishes of fruit with syrup are prepared, there is still the habit of guessing when the syrup is just right without using a thermometer. Another example is the continued use of whisks and beaters instead of mixers.

Regarding food preparation, the procedures are still somewhat rustic. For example, vegetables are peeled and cut without worrying much about removing every little bit of skin or making the pieces uniform in size. Steaks are of random size, some of them have bone pieces or even chips, and very often skin and gristle have not been removed. Within this framework of more or less rudimentary practices, it is very difficult to find a proper piece of meat where these parts have been removed, which in many South American countries is called a *despresado* of chicken, hen, duck, rabbit, and other edible animals. The same is true of beef joints.

These rudimentary practices do not result in dishes that are a delight to behold, although they can be very tasty. This is not only the case in a domestic setting, but also in many modest restaurants and some workplace cafeterias. Here, food is prepared as it has been done for time immemorial (i.e., without paying attention to the aesthetic factor). These rough cooking practices should not only be considered typical of the traditional South American cuisine, as they are also found in other places, including Europe. On the other hand, one cannot deny that the upper classes sometimes prove to be more careful when processing food ingredients, which results in a better presentation of the dishes.

The Urban World

The urban elements that have been incorporated into the culinary field of the region since the middle of the twentieth century are the result of technological modernization, infiltration of foreign foods and habits, and concern for nutrition and aesthetics. In the early twentieth century, the importation of appliances aimed at making the culinary work easier began to increase. Kerosene stoves began to be imported, followed by gas stoves and finally by electric stoves, marking the different stages of the contemporary evolution in this matter. Middle-aged South Americans are able to reconstruct the changes that have occurred since their childhood based on their memories of smells and sounds. They can remember their parents' kitchen, with clay and wooden pottery that made very different noises from those made by cooking pots and other metal utensils of more recent times. They could probably remember the monotonous sound of the pounding mortar or of the *metate* by listening to the shrillness produced by a blender. Similarly, they would be able to differentiate

Large wooden mortar (*pilón*).

the crackling of a wood fire from the warm silence of the gas flame or the electric stove.[7]

Importation and use of kerosene, gas, and electric stoves spread significantly throughout the continent after World War II. After the stove, the second most important modern electrical appliance that has been incorporated is probably the refrigerator. Since the 1950s, the refrigerator was used for water storing and cooling instead of the *tinajero*—a wooden cupboard, in which the filtering stone to obtain drinking water was placed, along with the earthen jar that would catch the water and the containers to serve and drink it.

Today, domestic and commercial South American kitchens are full of modern devices for food processing. These appliances not only make things easier for their users, but also save them time. Also, these items have been eradicating, although not completely, many beliefs regarding the skills of cooks. An example is the idea that certain people have a knack for beating a cake mixture or obtaining a smooth emulsion such as mayonnaise sauce. The Spanish expression for this is *tener buena mano*, which means "to have a skilled hand." Another key application of these modern devices, especially at home, is the cutting of uniform vegetable pieces. To a certain extent, electrical appliances have been successful because many traditional or typical regional dishes can be prepared using these devices, and often an accompanying cookbook shows how.

Of course, technological progress can also be seen in the wide range of canned, frozen, and vacuum-packed foods that can be stored in a pantry for a relatively long time, which changed the old habit of daily shopping. In the past, housewives had to go to the market every day to buy the ingredients they would use to prepare the meals of the day—a habit that even manifested in the colloquial Spanish expression *el diario* (literally "the everyday"), which corresponds to the day-to-day food expenses. Today, food shopping is done less often, thanks to the packaged and canned food and, of course, the fridge—especially its freezer section.

Another invention that appeared in South American kitchens in the second half of the twentieth century brought about significant changes to the practice of cooking, namely the microwave oven. Almost all South American households have one, even though some people are concerned about health effects.

With culinary modernization, typical dishes from other regions are now available in the market—frozen, canned, or packaged in any other form. So nowadays, in many cities of the continent, one can buy boxes with the ingredients to very quickly prepare a pizza, or cans that only have to be opened and heated in a double boiler (*en baño de María*) to make the Spanish bean stew called *fabada* or the French cassoulet, sparing oneself the difficulties and the time usually needed to prepare such dishes.

Modern dietary knowledge has also brought about certain changes in cooking, as the effort to avoid eating too much fat or sugar has resulted in some transformation of the traditional recipes, basically reducing the proportion of the ingredients that could be detrimental to one's health. Similarly, the importance given to the presentation of dishes has changed. The proper appearance and attractiveness of food are a main concern nowadays.

Another consequence of the saturation of modern technology in the kitchen is that many of the utensils that were used in the past for cooking

Grinding stone (*piedra de moler*).

are now only decorative elements. Especially in urban households and typical-food restaurants, it is common to find old pounding mortars now used as flower pots, as well as old grinding stones now used as mere decorative objects, creating an old atmosphere in modern kitchens.

Books on Food Culture

There is a large collection of books documenting the South American food culture, both cookbooks and books on the history, the folklore, and more.

Cookbooks

The publication of cookbooks began in the nineteenth century, but handwritten recipe books existed since long before and are still used today. Culinary titles are now considered a key field by the regional publishing houses. They have flooded the market with books, brochures, and magazines containing not only countless recipes, but also techniques, tricks, and general information on the topic, which are useful to both housewives and chefs.

Handwritten recipe books must be considered a highly useful source of information, as they really show what the actual domestic culinary practice is. These books are made based on a selection of recipes that have been either provided by relatives or friends or taken from books or any other written material and copied for everyday use. Cookbooks, by contrast, are mostly used as works of reference and reflect what could be called the ideal culinary practice, which does not always materialize. Both types of gastronomic information sources date far back. Handwritten notebooks are older than the cookbooks, and, in South America, some of the notebooks, dating back to the eighteenth century, still survive. It is not easy to find this type of handwritten material. They eventually get damaged or destroyed as a result of constant use and exposure to heat, as well as stains from the ingredients used for cooking. The few that still exist are jealously kept in the bosom of the families that made them.

The first printed cookbooks were published in the middle of the nineteenth century. It was only then that the recipes that made up the typical culinary heritage of each South American country were printed, becoming a sort of corpus representing the particular food cultures of each country. Some of the first well-known works of reference include the following. In Venezuela, *Cocina campestre*—as part of the work *El agricultor venezolano*, written by José A. Díaz—was published in 1861, and, three decades later, the book *Cocina criolla o guía del ama de casa*, written by Tulio Febres Cordero (Mérida, Venezuela: Tipografía El Lápiz), was published in 1899. In Colombia, a cookery handbook by an anonymous author came out in Bogotá in 1853 entitled *Manual de artes, oficios, cocina y repostería*, published by Nicolás Gómez Press. The third chapter of this book, devoted to cookery, was extracted from this first handbook and published as an independent book in 1874 by the same press under the title *Manual de cocina y repostería, conforme a los usos y a las costumbres de nuestro país y del extranjero*.

In Ecuador, the book *El cocinero práctico* was published in Quito in 1893—the author acknowledged under the initials A.G. In Peru, the handbook *Manual de buen gusto que facilita el modo de hacer los dulces, budines, colaciones y pastas y destruye los errores en tantas recetas mal copiadas* was printed in Arequipa in 1866, written by Valentín Ibáñez. In the same city, the third edition of the book *La mesa peruana o sea el libro de las familias precedido del arte de trinchar y de las reglas que deben observarse durante la comida*, an anonymous work, was published in 1867. In the second half of the nineteenth century, Juana Manuela Gorriti's work *Cocina ecléctica* (Buenos Aires: 1890) came out in Argentina. And finally, in Chile, Eulogio Martín's *Ciencia gastronómica (Recetas de guisos y potajes para postres)* was published in Santiago in 1851, the work *Cuaderno de guisos y postres* came out in Santiago in 1865, and—perhaps the most famous—*Manual del cocinero práctico*, written by Antonia and Isabel Errázuriz, was printed in Valparaíso in 1848. There were a number of editions of the latter, as well as a reprint entitled *Novísimo manual del cocinero práctico* (Santiago: 1896). In Brazil, the book *Cozinheiro Imperial ou Nova arte do cozinheiro e do copeiro em todos os seus ramos* was published in the early nineteenth century in Rio de Janeiro, the author concealing his or her identity through the initials M.R.C. Its second edition was printed in 1843, and the fifth in 1866—the latter being particularly interesting, as it featured typical recipes of the country that had not been included in the previous editions.

These books contain relatively substantial repertoires of what their authors considered to be the typical dishes of their respective countries, and, on the other hand, they also include a number of French-style dishes, because French cuisine had a great influence on the South American continent at the time. These old books still play an important role, as many dishes are prepared using the ingredients and methods originally presented. In fact, the recipes from a large number of contemporary cookbooks have practically been copied from the old ones, with just a few modifications. In other words, the old cookbooks are still part of the current food culture.

In the twentieth century, more and more cookbooks were published. The number of typical dishes they contained grew with time, some of them even only featuring very particular dishes that were typical of each of the countries. In most cases, especially until the 1950s, almost all recipes presented in such books were somewhat faulty, as they were not precise about the ingredients' measurements, used local terms that were unclear to nonnatives, lacked the ingredients' scientific names, and had other defects of this kind. By the 1980s and 1990s, though, the style was better and the content more precise. Cookbooks containing typical recipes were also published in languages other than Spanish, enabling a more effective and wider spread of the South American cuisine.

It is worth mentioning the most important cookbooks of some of the countries of the region. In Venezuela, there is *El libro de Tía María*, by María Chapellín, which was published for the first time in 1956, and *Mi cocina a la manera de Caracas*, by Armando Scannone, which came out in 1982 (both in Caracas); in Colombia, there is *Cartagena de Indias en la olla*, written by Teresita Román de Zurek and published in 1963, and *Gran libro de la cocina colombiana*, published in 1984 under the supervision of Fernando Wills (both in Bogotá); in Peru, there is *Comidas criollas peruanas*, by Francisca Baylon (n.d.), and *La gran cocina peruana*, by Jorge Stanbury, published in 1995 (both in Lima); in Brazil, there is *Dona Benta: Comer bem* (n.d.), published in São Paulo; in Argentina, there is *El libro de Doña Petrona*, written by Petrona C. de Gandulfo, published in 1907, with many editions (almost all of them in Buenos Aires); and in Chile, there is *La buena mesa*, by Olga Budge de Edwards, published in 1954 in Santiago de Chile.

This list was presented to illustrate the general scale, but the number of cookbooks that have been published in South America during the twentieth century is extremely large, especially if one takes into consideration those published since the 1980s, when a culinary publishing boom took place.

A key role in the spreading of information is played by periodicals, among which specialized magazines deserve to be mentioned: *Carta Blanca* and *Entremeses*, from Peru; *Cocina y Vinos* and *Zona Gourmet*, from Venezuela; *Gula*, from Brazil; *Cuisine and Vins*, from Argentina; *Vino Gourmand*, from Chile; *Bebidas y Manjares*, from Colombia; and *Cocina, Arte y Vida*, from Uruguay. The gastronomic sections of the main national newspapers of the different countries, or of the most widely broadcast magazines, are also important. These publications, which are more accessible to the masses, have significantly contributed both to the reinforcement of the culinary traditions and to the spreading of the modern techniques applied in the kitchen. Besides this, photographs have played a key role in this type of material and have led to the improvement of the dishes' presentation in the domestic setting.

The influence that culinary TV programs have had since the 1980s is also significant. These programs are broadcast on almost all the national channels of the region, as well as on foreign channels via satellite. This medium has aroused the South American public's interest in cooking to a greater extent than perhaps books and magazines. By teaching techniques applied in the most industrialized countries, as well as recipes from exotic countries, such programs have significantly stimulated South American modernization and creativity.

Finally, the great importance of the Internet, through which its users can obtain gastronomical information of any of the countries in a few seconds, must be acknowledged. Not only historical or cultural, but also practical data can be downloaded and accessed, including old and new recipes as well as many kinds of culinary techniques.

Academic Approaches

At the universities and other public and private educational institutes, special attention has been given to the study of food culture, primarily in the schools of hotel management and tourism, which have significantly developed since the 1980s. Two key examples of such an interest are the Escuela Profesional de Turismo y Hotelería (Professional School in Tourism and Hotel Management) at the Universidad San Martín de Porres, in Lima, Peru, and the Espacio Académico: Ciencia y Cultura de la Alimentación (Academic Space: Food Science and Culture) at the Universidad Nacional Experimental del Yaracuy, Venezuela. Important research work and diffusion of information on the topic are being carried out in both of these schools. In fact, the Universidad San Martín de Porres is noted for the publication of a vast number of culinary books. A number of researchers working for these institutions or freelancing have been researching the topic of food culture of their own countries for a considerable time. They have been publishing the results of their studies in the form of articles or books. The topics in such publications range from sociological or anthropological to nutritional matters, also including historical and folklore-related issues. In this sense, the relatively extensive literature on the topic proves that South Americans are more and more concerned about the origins and the evolution of their food.

As for the studies on food history, there are representative books in almost all South American countries. In Brazil, there is the book *História da Alimentação no Brasil*, written by Luís da Câmara Cascudo (2 vols., São Paulo: 1967); in Chile, *Apuntes para la historia de la cocina chilena*, by Eugenio Pereira Salas (Santiago: Editorial Universitaria, 1977); in Paraguay, *Panorama de la realidad histórica del Paraguay: Proceso de formación y evolución social del pueblo paraguayo a los fines nutricionales*, written by Francisco Américo Montalvo (La Asunción: 1967); in Peru, *La nutrición en el Antiguo Perú*, by Antúnez de Mayolo (Lima: Banco Central de Reserva del Perú, 1985), and the books *La cocina en el Virreinato del Perú* (Lima: Escuela Profesional de Turismo y Hotelería, Universidad San Martín de Porres, 1996) and *La cocina cotidiana y festiva de los limeños en el siglo XIX* (Lima: Escuela Profesional de Turismo y Hotelería, Universidad San Martín de Porres, 1999), both written by Rosario Oliva; in Colombia, the books *Historia de la cultura material en la América Equinoccial: la alimentación en Colombia y en los países vecinos*, written by Víctor Manuel Patiño (Bogotá: Biblioteca de la Presidencia de la República, 1984), and *Mesa y cocina en el siglo XIX*, by Aída Martínez Carreño (Bogotá: Fondo Cultural Cafetero, 1985); and, in Venezuela, *Historia de la alimentación en Venezuela*, by José Rafael Lovera (Caracas: Centro de Estudios Gastronómicos, 1998).

Food researchers are also coming together to exchange information. The *I Congreso sobre la preservación de las cocinas regionales de los países andinos* (First Congress on Preservation of the Andean Countries' Regional Cuisines)—called by the Universidad San Martín de Porres—was held in Lima, Peru, in 2003. A second congress of this kind will be held in 2005, in Santiago de Chile. This event is significant evidence that the research community devoted to the issue of food culture in South America is starting to institutionalize. Before 2003, specialists attended the congresses on Patrimonio Gastronómico y Turismo Cultural en América Latina y el Caribe (Culinary Heritage and Cultural Tourism in Latin America and the Caribbean) in Puebla, Mexico, the first of which was held in 1999. The fifth congress was held in 2004, but the first one specifically devoted to the South American continent was the one held in Peru in 2003.[8] Among the topics discussed in all of these congresses are the role of cooks, culinary education, features of the culinary literature, history of cooking as a trade, and its current and future challenges.

Toward a New South American Cuisine?

A number of elements are paving the way for the emergence of new trends in the culinary field, the most important being the accelerated urbanization experienced by the countries of the region to a greater or lesser extent, the globalization phenomenon, and the resurgence of the attempts to preserve national cultural features. Many young people who became cooks and chefs during the 1980s and 1990s and learned the modern cooking techniques are now giving free rein to their creativity by taking advantage of the knowledge they have acquired and investigating native ingredients to reinterpret the old recipes and invent new ones. Some of these young chefs brought their ideas to fruition by establishing restaurants in cities such as New York and Miami with the objective of attracting a new public with their cuisine. Others stayed in their native countries and devoted themselves to offering their compatriots and the visitors coming from the main South American cities both their new versions of the traditional dishes and the results of their creative cuisine. The chefs abroad have been quite successful, especially because of the exotic nature of the cuisine they offer. Those who stayed have had to fight against a culinary orthodoxy that is not easy to overcome. Most South Americans—accustomed to the traditional presentation of dishes and to the habitual use of certain ingredients—have rejected this new type of cuisine. Nevertheless, urbanites, who have become familiar with the contemporary cuisine, as they usually travel to other countries and often visit foreign restaurants—especially French ones—are now more open to the new offerings. Besides, as the behavior of this kind of elite has always been a model to be followed, their acceptance of this new trend has helped to overcome the rejection by the masses little by little. In any case, a new trend is already taking shape, which can be understood as the emergence of a new South American cuisine.

This new trend is evolving along different paths, as a result of the different degrees of nationalism featured by the chefs. Some try to present the typical dishes in an innovative—sometimes even avant-garde—way, but are careful to retain their authenticity so as to be familiar to the palate. Other chefs, foreign-born or of foreign ancestry, try to combine their own culinary traditions with that of the country in which they work, allowing for a new kind of mixing process. The best example is perhaps the so-called *nikei* cuisine, which is a mixture of Japanese and Peruvian cuisines. The results of this combination are incredibly original, enabling this cuisine to become one of Peru's gastronomical epitomes and tourist attractions. Another group of chefs create new dishes by using ingredients that are native to the South American countries. The dishes they create have sometimes been so successful that they could be considered brand products. Even though these groups are evolving in different directions and pursuing different goals, there is no doubt that, as a whole, they all are clear signs that a new South American cuisine is emerging.

NOTES

1. Antonio Castillo de Lucas, *Refranerillo de la alimentación* (Madrid: Gráficas Reunidas, S. A., 1940), pp. 52, 129. See also José Deleito y Piñuela, *La mujer, la casa y la moda* (Madrid: Espasa Calpe, 1946).

2. Guillermo Furlong, *Historia social y cultural del Río de la Plata*, vol. 2, *El transplante social* (Buenos Aires: Tipográfica Editora Argentina, 1969), p. 353.

3. Ibid.

4. José Rafael Lovera, *Manuel Guevara Vasconcelos o la política del convite* (Caracas: Academia Nacional de la Historia, 1998), p. 45.

5. Quoted in ibid., p. 31.

6. Simón B. O'Leary, ed., *Memorias del General O'Leary publicadas por su hijo*, vol. 24 (Caracas: Imprenta de El Monitor, 1884), p. 14.

7. José Rafael Lovera, *Historia de la alimentación en Venezuela* (Caracas: Centro de Estudios Gastronómicos, 1998), p. 203.

8. The memoirs of these congresses, containing material related to Venezuela, Colombia, Brazil, Peru, Chile, and Argentina, have been all published in Mexico by CONACULTA—those from the three first congresses in 2002 (in three volumes), and those from the fourth congress in 2003.

4

Typical Meals

Daily mealtimes have followed a relatively similar pattern for the last five centuries in South America. In the urban context, at least three meals have always been eaten, while in the rural context, just two is normal. The three main meals eaten in cities are designated as *desayuno* (breakfast), *almuerzo* or *comida* (lunch), and *cena* (dinner). Another one can be added to these, called *merienda* (snack). In the rural context, the meals are called *desayuno* and *cena*. Mealtimes have always been related to the daily work schedule. In the case of urban dwellers, there is a deeply rooted habit of having a break at noon, which has become so important that it even had to be acknowledged by labor laws. Even though these patterns are found throughout South America, the mealtimes sometimes change from one country to another. In Venezuela and Colombia, for instance, breakfast is generally consumed very early in the morning, between 7 and 8 A.M.; lunch takes place between 12 and 1 or 1:30 P.M.; and dinner is eaten between 8 and 9 P.M. The farmers living in these two countries have breakfast even earlier, usually between 5 and 6 A.M., and their second meal is eaten around 6 P.M. More to the south, the mealtimes are different. For example, in urban Chile and Argentina these three meals are consumed at least one hour later than in Venezuela and Colombia; however, in northern Chile and Argentina, farmers eat their meals at very early hours, just like the Venezuelan and Colombian ones. The so-called *merienda*, which is not necessarily eaten every day, in the urban context occurs between 4 and 5 P.M. In general terms, this meal is typically eaten by children, and not so much by adults. It can be said that the accelerated pace of life in contemporary times has resulted in the prevalence of breakfast and dinner as the most important mealtimes.

In Venezuela, the three essential meals have been designated as *los tres golpes* (literally "the three hits"). This expression of the everyday language is used to refer to people's purchasing power. So those people with the less financial resources are said *que no tienen para los tres golpes* (not to be able to afford the three meals). In other countries, like Argentina, food is referred to as *el puchero* (the stew), so there will be people who *no les alcanza para completar el puchero* (cannot even afford the stew). A great variety of dishes can be prepared for each of these meals. Thus, only some illustrative examples will be presented.

BREAKFAST

The first meal of the day, breakfast (*desayuno* or *pequeno almoço*), is bread-based. There is a very wide range of bread types, as there are different ingredients that can be used to make it, different means of obtaining these ingredients, and various ways to prepare and consume the bread. Even though the concept of bread is univocal and universal inasmuch as this product is essential to human beings, detailed research on the different cultures shows that the concept actually becomes diverse and specific. The European conquerors of the sixteenth century used the word almost exclusively to refer to wheat bread, but for the contemporaneous native peoples of the Americas, bread was made from corn or cassava. Many African slaves, though, considered plantains to be their bread.

The typical South American types—mainly based on the use of corn and cassava (or manioc)—are discussed here first, then the wheat breads, and finally the plantain-based types. Although corn and cassava or manioc breads dominate, consumption statistics indicate that wheat bread has been playing an ever more considerable role. Another very important element of South American breakfasts is coffee, which is consumed either alone or with milk.

Breads

Corn

From north to south, the most important corn breads are *arepas* (from Venezuela and part of Colombia) and tamales (found in the rest of the continent), plus a variety of the tamales known as *humita*.

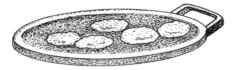

Arepas on a griddle (*budare*).

An *arepa* is a patty of about 10 to 15 cm (about 5 inches) in diameter and 1 to 3 cm (3/4 inch) thick, made with corn flour, no yeast, and
sometimes even without salt. Making *arepas* involves removing the corn
kernels from the corncobs, which, once soaked, would be ground in the
metate or in the *pilón*. Then, the dough obtained is shaped into patties
by pressing small amounts of dough against the palms of both hands.
These small patties are cooked over a flame on a griddle, which used to
be made of clay and is now made of iron. This griddle has been recently
substituted by a kind of waffle iron made of cast iron, and lately some
industries are even manufacturing an electrical appliance that serves the
same purpose. Nowadays, the food industry produces a precooked corn
flour that saves people all the hard work that is required to obtain the
dough. This product has enabled the successful survival of this dish that
dates back to pre-Columbian times and that still plays a role within the
hectic everyday life of contemporary times. *Arepas* must be eaten when
they are freshly cooked, or they will go stale; reheating them does not
work well, and they tend to become moldy quickly. This South American
bread is more or less the equivalent of the hoecake, which was shaped
similarly to the *arepa*, used to be eaten during colonial times in the southern United States, and named for the process the African slaves used to
cook the corn dough. The name *arepa* derives from the Carib word *erepa*,
which appears in the vocabularies written by the Spanish missionaries of
colonial times as an equivalent of food, sustenance, or bread, and which
in turn derives from the word *aripo*, which was used to refer to the round
griddle used by the natives to cook the bread. It would seem that the
Cumanagoto tribe inhabiting the northeastern part of what is now Venezuela were the ones who started to use the word *arepa* to designate this
corn-based patty—a term that then spread throughout the rest of the
Venezuelan territory as well as in Colombia.

Arepas are always part of everyday breakfasts and can also be eaten
throughout the day, as in many cities they are eaten for lunch, filled with
cheese, stewed meat, chicken, or beans, with ground pork cracklings sometimes added to the dough. Such preparations have very picturesque names,

like the one used in Venezuela to refer to *arepas* filled with stewed chicken and pieces of avocado, namely *reina pepiada*, which would be something like "saucy queen," or the term used to designate *arepas* filled with black beans and white cheese, namely *dominó*. *Arepas* can be considered the fast food of the inhabitants of these regions. Even though this bread is commonly cooked on a griddle, in Colombia it is sometimes fried in oil. Another remarkable aspect includes the fact that *arepas* are also prepared adding grated brown sugarloaf (i.e., unrefined sugar) and aniseeds to the dough. This type of *arepa* is consumed as an afternoon snack with grated white fresh cheese.

Cornmeal has also been used to prepare other types of small breads, with an elongated instead of a round shape, known as tamales. They are not only typical of South America, but are also a key feature of the food culture of other regions, such as Mexico. The general term used to refer to these corn breads is native to the Central American territory, specifically deriving from the Nahuatl language, in which they were called *tamalli*—a term that was then spread by the conquerors throughout the rest of the New World. In the Andean region, within the territory that once corresponded to the Inca Empire, they were designated with the Quechua word *humintas*, which is still used in Peru, Bolivia, and Chile. However, in this same area, people differentiate between tamales and *humintas* today, the main difference being the fact that the former are made with dried and cooked corn and the latter with fresh corn (called *jojoto* in Venezuela and *choclo* in Peru). Besides, there are different types of tamales depending on their filling, ranging from the Venezuelan *hallaca*—consisting of corn dough filled with a stew made of pork, hen, and even beef, plus other ingredients—to the Peruvian tamale, whose filling is only a piece of pork dewlap and a black olive. The Venezuelan *hallaca* and Peruvian tamales are wrapped in plantain leaves, while the others are wrapped in the same corn husks. South American tamales are boiled and not steamed, as is the case of the Central American ones. The varieties of tamales that are considered in order to classify them as breads are those prepared only with the corn dough (i.e., those without fillings). There are sweet and also savory tamales, while some are simply neutral tasting. They are eaten for breakfast, as snacks, or sometimes are even served for lunch or dinner as an accompaniment to heavy stews. In Brazil, a variety of tamale called *pamonhas* is sweetened with sugar, and grated coconut and cassava are added. *Pamonhas* are typical of Bahia, Paraiba, Recife, and Ceara.

Humitas (Bolivia)

- 10 ears of fresh corn and their husks
- 1 1/2 tablespoons sugar
- 3 eggs
- 2 pounds cheese, grated
- 1/4 cup lard
- 1/4 cup butter
- salt to taste

Remove the husks and set aside. Grate the raw corn and mix it with the beaten eggs. Melt lard and butter and add them to the mixture. Add the cheese, sugar, and salt. Mix everything well and place spoonfuls of the mixture in the corn husks. Close them by doubling the husk. Tie them in the middle. Cook (preferably steam) for 1 hour. (10 to 12 servings)

Cassava or Manioc

Another bread type that is traditionally prepared in the tropical zone of South America since pre-Hispanic times is the *casabe*. There is also the so-called *mañoco*—another food consumed as bread and typical of Amazonia. The *casabe* is a big, round, flat bread made from bitter cassava, which is previously grated and pressed to obtain a mixture that is spread with a wooden spatula on a round griddle (made of clay in the past and of iron nowadays) called a *budare*, *aripo*, or *callana*. This bread is not seasoned, so its flavor is simply that of the tuber used to prepare it. The diameter of this sort of pancake or cracker ranges approximately from 40 to 60 centimeters (15 to 25 inches), and it is usually no thicker than half a centimeter (1/4 inch). As it is impossible to serve a cracker of this size on a table, it is usually broken up into four or more pieces, which is done by pressing on the bread with the side of the hand. Nevertheless, smaller *casabes* of five to six centimeters (about 2.25 inches) in diameter are being produced in the main Venezuelan and Colombian cities, and are served along with other breads like *arepas* and tamales. There are basically two types of *casabe:* a thicker one, which is difficult to break and also to chew, which is usually soaked in broth or water when it is on the table, and a thinner type, which can thus be easily broken and was called a *xau-xau* in the past and a *galleta* (cracker) today. The thicker type of *casabe* was consumed in pre-Columbian times by the tribe chiefs and witch doctors. *Mañoco* is also obtained by pressing grated cassava, but it is then only toasted a little on the griddle and stirred to obtain a kind of lumpy and dry starch. This food is used as an accompaniment to stews, just as if it were, for example, rice. In contemporary times, cassava flour is commonly used to prepare some kinds of *arepas* or small tamales.

Other Breads of Wheat or Plantain

Even though neither wheat nor plantains are native to South America, their early transfer to the region, plus the European and African influence, paved the way for breads based on the use of these ingredients to be accepted and to become popular. The bread made with wheat flour, taken to South America by the conquerors, was soon appreciated, and with time its consumption spread throughout the region, to the extent that currently it is very popular and competes—sometimes quite successfully—with the South American breads. There is a very wide range of these breads, not only because of the different regions where they are prepared, but also due to the differences arising from the seasons of the year in which they are made, which will be described in chapter 6, "Special Occasions." Generally speaking, though, loaves of bread similar to the French baguette or to the Galician bread types are prepared in Venezuela, as well as certain round bread rolls seasoned with unrefined sugar and aniseeds called *acemitas*, which are native to the Andean region of that country. In Colom-

Bread sellers, one drinking *mate*, Caacupe, Paraguay. © TRIP/M. Barlow.

bia, both in Cundinamarca and in Boyacá, *mogolla* is prepared, which is a bread made with wheat bran, while in Popayán, *pambazo* is prepared—a bread loaf made with whole wheat flour, yeast, eggs, salt, sugar, lard, and lukewarm water. Currently, the bread-making industry has gained considerable importance in the entire continent. Almost every food store sells loaves, which are made in the American style, bringing about the popularization of the electrical appliances that toast them.

Plantains are also used to prepare dishes that take the role of bread. The unripe fruit is sliced into very thin rounds and fried, receiving the name *tostones* in Venezuela. In Colombia, a similar dish is prepared, the *patacones*, which consist of thicker slices that are first mashed, then fried and sometimes seasoned with garlic. In some tropical zones, the role of bread is also played by balls made with cooked and mashed plantains, which are known as *bolas de plátano*. These plantain balls have been traditionally associated with the slave population and are only eaten in rural areas today.

Egg Dishes

Eggs are constantly present in South American breakfasts. They can be served in different forms: fried, scrambled, or as omelets. Scrambled eggs can include onions, chives, and chopped tomatoes—in which case the dish is called *perico* in Venezuela. Omelets can feature onions, tomatoes, and also diced fresh cheese, as well as pork chorizo sausage, and are usually seasoned with cumin and salt.

Fruit

Fruit is generally eaten for breakfasts, but it can also be part of lunch. The range of fruits with which nature has provided South America is incredibly wide. Therefore, there are countless fruit dishes in the different continental zones, so only a few examples will be presented. To this end, two key fruits have been chosen for being the most prestigious ones within the regional cuisine, namely avocados and plantains. The *ensalada de aguacate* (avocado salad) is one good example. It is served either as a starter or as a side, especially with grilled meat. Its preparation involves cutting the avocado pulp in segments that are then seasoned with oil, vinegar, and onions, plus salt, pepper, and sometimes hot pepper. Another well-known dish made with this fruit is the *aguacate relleno* (stuffed avocados), which came about because of the ease with which the fruit can be cut into half lengthwise (without peeling it), the big pit removed, and then each half stuffed with a salad made of shrimp, crab, or chicken mixed with mayonnaise sauce, and generally garnished with parsley. This is a starter in almost all South American restaurants but is also prepared at home.

Plantains are also a common food in South America, especially in the tropical region. One famous plantain dish used as accompaniment is prepared by removing the skins, cutting them only a little lengthwise and filling them with butter and fresh cheese, wrapping them in wax paper or tinfoil, and finally oven roasting them. Another way to prepare them is by slicing the ripe fruit on the diagonal and frying them. They can also be used to prepare the typical dishes known as *tostones* and *patacores* mentioned earlier.

Beverages

The alcohol-free beverages of choice in South America, generally available for breakfast, are coffee and cocoa. Coffee plays a much more important role than cocoa. Coffee has become the national beverage of Brazil and Colombia (large coffee producers) and also of Venezuela (a minor producer). This does not imply that coffee is a common beverage in only these three countries. It is actually consumed in the whole region every morning before work, both in the country and in the city; during a break at work; and after dinner. The South American coffee production is not only one of the largest in the world, but also one with the highest quality, as Colombia and Venezuela have fine Arabica-type coffee beans that successfully compete with coffee beans from other world regions. Cocoa, which played the main role up until the nineteenth century, has not completely vanished in contemporary times, probably thanks to the fact that the chocolate industry produces soluble cacao powder in large quantities, providing for a very popular product that is even imported by other countries, especially the United States. Cocoa is nowadays consumed either hot or cold.

There are other typical beverages in the region that, depending on their preparation, can be classified as alcohol-free or as alcoholic drinks. First of all, there is *chicha*, which is consumed in the whole Andean region and in Amazonia. This beverage is mostly prepared with corn, but sometimes it is also made with cassava or with rice. Corn *chicha*—one of the most important legacies of pre-Colombian Indians—continues to be very appreciated by many people. Its preparation varies depending on the country, but a common procedure is followed everywhere: corn is ground and left to ferment with some water, to which other ingredients are added, such as pineapple peels and some unrefined cane sugar. During the first half of the twentieth century, the consumption of this strongly fermented drink was so high that it even became prohibited by the law, as its consumption was considered a cause of alcoholism among the indigenous populations. This was the case particularly in Colombia. Other drinks are designated as *chicha*, but they are not made with corn, as is the case of *cachirri*, which is made with fermented cassava, in the Amazonian region, and which is practically only consumed by native tribes still living in these vast areas, as well as by some *criollos* living there, who have become accustomed to drinking it. In Venezuela and Colombia, a drink called *chicha* is prepared with rice and aromatized with almond essence. Even though this rice *chicha* is slightly fermented, it cannot be considered an alcoholic drink. In these two countries, this beverage is industrially produced and sold in all supermarkets, while there are still vendors called *chicheros* selling it on the street.

Within this subclass of alcohol-free beverages, there is a drink that is more liquid than *chicha*, consisting of unrefined sugar or brown sugarloaf diluted in water with some lime. This refreshing liquid is known in the Colombian-Venezuelan Andean zone as *agua de panela, papelón con limón, aguamiel*, and also *guarapo*. It is consumed either raw or cooked depending on the locale. Sometimes pineapple peels are added to this *guarapo*, resulting in certain fermentation.

Other typical alcohol-free beverages are the fruit drinks, designated as *frescos, caratos*, or *batidos*. These are prepared with tropical fruits like papaya, guava, mango, pineapple, and soursop, among many others, and are sweetened with cane sugar. Sometimes, different fruits are mixed to obtain new flavors. In South America, these drinks still compete with carbonated beverages, among which there are some that are native to the region, such as Inca Cola or Guaraná.

LUNCH

Despite the limitations imposed by the accelerated pace of contemporary life on lunch (*almuerzo* or *almoço*), it can still be said that for South Americans there is no lunch if there is no soup. Pots and soups play a very important role in South American cuisine, most of them stemming from their analogous European dishes. The habit of eating soup as the first course in a meal is deeply rooted among South Americans, so the homes and restaurants where they are not offered should be considered exceptions. Very often, it is even the case that soup is the only thing served, especially in a poorer household. If suddenly more people come to the house at mealtimes, there will not be any problem in receiving them and giving them something to eat if there is a soup, as some water could simply be added to it—as an old popular saying states—so that there is enough for everybody. There are countless types of soups, because the ingredients that are normally available to the people in the markets and any other food stores can be combined in innumerable ways. Some representative ones will be described here.

South American Pots

The pots prepared in South America basically stem from the food culture of both pre-Columbian natives and the Europeans that conquered and colonized the new lands. The Carib indigenous people used to prepare a kind of soup that was very hot, using hot peppers, water, certain herbs, and pieces of game meat. This sort of concoction is still consumed in some Caribbean islands, where it is called "Caribbean pot," and in the Guianas, where it is called "pepper pot." As for the Iberian influence, South American pots are reminiscent of the famous *olla podrida* that appears in the Spanish and Portuguese recipe books of the European contact period. The *olla podrida* can be considered the mother of many of the soups consumed in the different South American countries. Some of its South American offshoots are the Venezuelan *hervidos* and *sancochos*, based on the use of stocks of beef, poultry, or fish; the Colombian *ajiaco* and other Colombian soups also known as *sancochos*; the Brazilian *cozido*; and the Argentinean *puchero*. The *puchero* is the one most similar to the Iberian pot.

Puchero (Argentina)

- 2 pounds beef short ribs
- 1/2 pound lean and salted pork, sliced
- 1 1/2 pounds chicken, cut into pieces
- 3 Spanish chorizo sausages
- 4 quarts water
- 6 peeled carrots
- 6 medium onions

- 6 cloves garlic, chopped
- 1 small squash, peeled, cleaned, and sliced
- 6 tomatoes
- 1 cabbage, vertically cut into eight parts
- 1 green pepper, seeded
- 6 medium potatoes, peeled
- 6 leeks, cut into 3-inch pieces
- 1 16-ounce can chickpeas, drained
- 2 tablespoons parsley, finely chopped

Fill a large pot with 4 quarts of water, bring to a boil, and add the beef, pork, and chicken. Put the lid on the pot and cook over medium heat for 1 1/2 hours. Add the chorizos and carrots and cook for 30 minutes more. Add the onions, garlic, squash, tomatoes, cabbage, green pepper, potatoes, leeks, chickpeas, and parsley. Continue cooking for 30 minutes more until potatoes are tender. Remove the meat and arrange on a platter. Do the same with the vegetables, placing them around the meat. Serve the broth in soup dishes and bring everything to the table. Each person will help him or herself directly from the platter. (10 to 12 servings)

This sort of "offspring" of the Iberian pot is generally characterized by the use of South American vegetables, such as cassava, taro, *arracacha*, sweet potatoes, corncobs, and an ingredient of African origin, the yam. An example of these kinds of soups is the *ajiaco bogotano*.

Ajiaco Bogotano (Colombia)

- 1 large chicken
- 6 small yellow potatoes
- 1 cup butter
- 3 large onions, finely chopped
- 1/4 cup capers
- 8 medium white potatoes
- 6 cups chicken stock
- 1 teaspoon salt
- 1/4 teaspoon ground pepper
- 3 *guasca* leaves (optional)
- 3 tender corncobs, cut into halves

Cut up the chicken into pieces and season it with salt and pepper. In a pot, brown the chicken in butter. Add the onions and stir to keep it from burning. Pour in the chicken stock and let boil. Slice half of the white potatoes and add to thicken the stock, along with the corncob halves. Let boil until all the ingredients are well cooked. Dice the remaining white potatoes and add along with the yellow ones (whole). Cook until tender, which means the soup is ready. Add the capers and *guasca* leaves just before serving. (6 servings)

Sometimes, the stocks made with beef, fish, or certain sea products are thickened with milk, and fresh cheese and eggs are added. These soups are called *chupe* and are equivalent to the American chowders. In the Andean zone, and particularly in Peru, *chupe de camarones* (shrimp chowder) is very popular; this soup is usually hot, as chopped hot peppers or chili paste is added.

Chupe de Camarones (Peru)

- 2 cups shrimp, peeled
- 2 pounds white-fleshed fish, cut into medium-sized pieces
- 1 pound potatoes, peeled, water-boiled, and chopped into large pieces
- 1 cup peas
- 1 pound rice
- 4 cups milk
- 3 eggs, beaten
- 1 cup vegetable fat
- 1 onion, chopped
- 6 tomatoes, peeled and diced
- 2 red peppers, seeded and diced
- 1 cup white cheese, diced
- salt, pepper, and oregano to taste

Brown the onions in preheated fat. Add the tomatoes and one of the red peppers, and cook for about 15 minutes. Add the potatoes and peas. Then add the milk and the rice and stir well. Season to taste with salt, pepper, and oregano. Cook for 15 to 20 minutes. Add the other red pepper, the fish, and the beaten eggs. Let it cook for 15 minutes more. Remove from heat and add the cheese just before serving. (6 to 8 servings)

In Venezuela, *chupe de gallina* (hen chowder), which does not have eggs but does have asparagus, is prepared.

Varied Soups

Many other soups are prepared throughout the continent, such as the green plantain soup, which is not only consumed by adults, but especially given to the kids when they have an upset stomach, due to its binding properties—something like the Iberian apple compote. The repertoire of South American soups also features countless preparations based on beans. The beans are stewed and then either left whole or reduced to a puree that is then diluted with stock. Some examples would be the white-bean and the green-bean soups—both from Antioquia, Colombia—based on the use of pork stock. There is also the *chupe de porotos* (Chilean bean chowder), considered one of the top dishes of Chilean cuisine, which includes celery, bay leaves, red pepper, garlic, ginger, and tomatoes and is dyed with saffron (diluted with sherry) or ground Spanish paprika. Another example is the *sopa de feijão preto* (Brazilian black-bean soup); a ham bone is used to prepare the stock, to which hot pepper is added, as well as leeks, onions, celery, cumin, cloves, chopped-up hard-boiled eggs, lime slices, and sometimes cream and some wine.

Not all South American soups are prepared using multiple ingredients, though. People also consume soups like consommé, especially the one made from hen, which has been always known for its invigorating properties and was therefore given for 40 consecutive days to women who had just given birth. So when a man would find out that his wife was pregnant, he would start to set aside enough money to be able to buy 40 hens, so that she could follow such a diet. (This practice is still carried out in the rural areas.) Besides, hen consommé has played an important role in wakes, as it is served to the deceased's relatives and friends to keep them awake. Of course, this soup was also consumed in other occasions, especially at important dinners where this dish would contribute certain elegance.

Many times, soup is the only dish eaten at lunch. Yet it can be followed by a dish with beef or fish, or also with vegetables, like rice—usually accompanied by beans and fried plantains, as is the case of the Venezuelan dish called *pabellón*:

Pabellón (Venezuela)

Beans
- 1 pound black beans
- 1 tablespoon brown sugar
- 3 tablespoons vegetable oil

- 1/2 medium red pepper, cut in strips
- 1 medium onion, finely chopped
- 1/2 teaspoon salt
- 1/8 teaspoon cumin
- 2 cloves garlic, finely chopped

Rice
- 2 cups rice
- 4 cups water
- 3 tablespoons vegetable oil
- 2 cloves garlic
- 1/2 medium onion
- 1/2 teaspoon salt
- 1/2 large red pepper

Fried Meat
- 1 pound flank
- 1 clove garlic, finely chopped
- 1/2 large onion, peeled and finely chopped
- 1/2 cup vegetable oil
- 2 tomatoes, peeled and diced
- 1/4 tablespoon salt

Plantains
- 2 ripe plantains
- 1/4 cup oil

Beans. Wash beans well and soak overnight. The next day, boil in water until soft. Make a *sofrito* with the onions, garlic, salt, cumin, and pepper. Add this *sofrito* to the soft beans and mix in brown sugar. Stir carefully and let boil over medium heat until it thickens.

Rice. Rinse the rice well. Boil the water with the condiments. Add the rice. Let it boil until the water starts to reduce. Turn heat to very low and cover the pot. Remove from heat when the grain is puffy.

Fried meat. Boil the meat with salt until it is tender. Drain the water and shred the meat. In a frying pan, sauté the onion, tomatoes, and garlic for 15 minutes to prepare a *sofrito*. Add the shredded meat and mix well. Continue frying for 15 minutes more.

Plantains. Peel and cut the ripe plantains diagonally into 1/4-inch-thick slices. Fry them in very hot oil.

Place each element on a separate serving dish. People will serve themselves a portion of each ingredient, which they will mix or eat alternately. (6 servings)

DINNER

Dinner (*cena* or *jantar*) is probably the most important meal of the day in the continent. Some of the typical dishes that can be featured by this meal are presented here.

Stews, Fried Food, Roasts, and Salads

Meat

Even though the South American food culture features a wide range of meats and meat-based recipes, there are three main classes: beef, pork, and poultry. It is remarkable that the prices of these very meat types have considerably increased since the early 1990s. The highest price increase has been for beef and pork. Poultry can still be afforded by the majority of the population. Most of the recipes used to prepare meat have Spanish roots, although some of them are pre-Columbian recipes that have evolved with the incorporation of foreign ingredients or European ways of cooking.

The beef-based dishes can be classified in two main categories: those prepared outside and those prepared in the kitchen. The best examples of

Parrilla—sheep barbecue, Tierra del Fuego, Argentina. © TRIP/Eric Smith.

those made outside are probably the *ternera llanera*, typical of Venezuela, and the Argentinean roast (*asado*). Both have been traditionally prepared by the inhabitants of the Llanos and Pampas and involve the use of more than one freshly obtained piece of meat and sometimes the whole animal. The cooking procedure is relatively easy: first, a sizable bonfire should be lit; then, when the embers have formed, metal or hard wooden sticks must be driven into the pieces of meat and placed around the embers. The meat is not seasoned; only a little salt is added when the meat is ready—mostly when it is very well done. Those who will eat the meat (traditionally, the Venezuelan *llaneros* and the Brazilian, Uruguayan, and Argentinean gauchos), armed with very sharp knives, cut the parts they feel like eating and take them with their hands to bring them directly to their mouths. Others will have their pieces cut and served in a wooden tray or on a pewter or china plate, and use a knife and their hands to cut and eat the meat. This is said to be the traditional and authentic way to prepare and consume a roast. These roasts are usually eaten without side dishes, although sometimes they can be accompanied by certain corn-bread rolls, *casabe*, or any boiled tuber. Nowadays, there are restaurants known as *parrilladas* or *churrascarias* in almost all South American countries where people can consume such roasts ready made. These places are even endowed with smoke extractors, which are not always as efficient as they should be, as the clients' clothes usually end up smelling of *parrilla* (roast). This dish has become very popular in almost all South American cities, and different varieties have emerged in different places. An example of such an evolution is the case of the Argentinean-style restaurants that were established in Venezuela in the middle of the twentieth century. They only served meat in the beginning but soon began to add other dishes, such as boiled cassava, corn-bread rolls called *hallaquitas*, *arepas*, fresh cheese, and a sauce called *guasacaca* made of avocado and herbs, which is native to Venezuela, as well as another hot sauce prepared with hot pepper. Moreover, this Venezuelan version of the Argentinean *parrillada* eliminated the entrails served in Argentina and replaced them with sausages and chorizos. This is, in fact, a very peculiar example of the Argentinean roast's transculturation.

Meat is also prepared in the kitchen. There are countless dishes prepared there, and they vary depending on the part of the animal that is being used and the cooking method applied. In Argentina—to start with the country whose cattle is the most famous—there is a very popular dish called *matambre*, made with the flank (i.e., the cut taken from between the rib bones and the skin of the animal). This cut (also known as *mat-*

ambre in Spanish) is seasoned with salt, pepper, hot pepper, some oil and vinegar, parsley, and bay leaves. The whole piece is then rolled, tied with a string, wrapped up in wax paper, placed in a container, and roasted. Then, when it is ready, it is cut into slices that can be served with different side dishes. In Colombia, especially in the area of Cundinamarca, the same meat cut, known as *sobrebarriga*, is used to make a dish with the same name. Preparing it involves boiling the meat for a long period of time to tenderize it; seasoning the water with onions, garlic, oregano, thyme, bay leaves, coriander, and other herbs; and then draining the meat and roasting it after marinating it with bitter beer. It is usually served with potatoes or rice. In Peru, the typical dish is the *anticuchos*, which are chunks of cattle heart marinated with vinegar, hot pepper, garlic, and other condiments and then skewered and grilled. Peruvians are very keen on preparing this dish, which is not only offered in almost all inexpensive restaurants, but also in food stands on the street. In Venezuela, people usually consume the *falda* (skirt) cut, which is almost equivalent to the cut known as *matambre* in Argentina. It is first boiled, then shredded and cut into 5 to 8 cm (about 2.5 inches) long strips, and finally stewed using the *sofrito* sauce as a base.

In Uruguay, the popular meat dish is the *carbonada*. It is prepared with veal that is cut in small cubes and browned in the pot where the *sofrito* has been prepared; then different vegetables are added, and when everything is tender, peach and apple pieces are added, as well as rice. This is left on the stove until the rice is cooked.

Carbonada (Uruguay)

- 1 pound veal meat
- 3 peaches, peeled, pitted, and diced
- 1/2 cup oil
- 3 tablespoons stock
- 1 tablespoon vegetable fat
- 1 medium onion, peeled and finely chopped
- 3/4 cup squash, peeled and diced
- 2 tomatoes, peeled and diced
- 2 corncobs, cut into halves
- 3/4 cup rice, cooked
- 1 medium potato, peeled and diced
- 1 apple, peeled, seeded and diced

- 2 cloves garlic
- 1 sweet potato, peeled and diced
- 1/8 teaspoon oregano
- 1/8 teaspoon thyme
- 1/8 teaspoon bay leaves
- 1/2 tablespoon parsley
- 1/4 tablespoon salt

Dice the meat. Sauté garlic and onions, add the meat, and let brown. Add the tomatoes, fat, and herbs. Add the vegetables to the meat. Season with salt and pepper. Cover and let cook over low heat until tender. Add peaches, apple, and rice. Cover again and put on low heat for 15 minutes more. (6 servings)

In Chile, the most highly prized meat-based dish is the empanada, which consists of a wheat pastry that is filled with a stew made from small pieces of meat, carrots, black olives, raisins, and hard-boiled eggs and seasoned with celery, oregano, onions, cumin, and hot pepper. It is not fried, but roasted, unlike many other empanadas.

Pork is very popular in South America, which is the best proof of the great influence exerted by the Iberian cuisine in the region. Practically all the dishes prepared with pork have an Iberian origin, which becomes clear if one takes a look at their names: *jamón, chicharrón,* chorizos, *longanizas,* and *morcillas,* among others. No matter where it is raised and consumed, nothing goes to waste from this generous animal, because what is not used for eating is used for something else. The hams that used to be prepared in Spain and Portugal before the conquest are considered the ancestors of some of the South American hams, like the Venezuelan *pernil* and the Peruvian *jamón del país.* The *pernil* consists of a leg of pork marinated in garlic, vinegar, oregano, and cumin, which is then roasted in the oven until golden brown on the outside and juicy on the inside. It is prepared for certain special occasions and is presented in slices, drizzled with the cooking juices. These slices are also used to prepare a sandwich made with small, elongated wheat-bread buns—a kind of snack that is served in many restaurants along Venezuelan roads. The *jamón del país,* native to Peru, is a similar dish that is also prepared with the leg of the pork, but is boiled in water instead of roasted. It is previously seasoned with cumin, hot pepper, oil, and pepper; tightly wrapped in a piece of fabric; and tied with a string. It is eaten as a main course, presented in slices, or used to fill sandwiches, in which pieces of black olives and a sauce made with thinly cut onions, hot pepper, and lime are also added.

A special snack that is appreciated in practically all South American countries is the *chicharrón*, which requires frying and then sprinkling of salt. It is usually eaten while having a couple of drinks or simply as a snack. In some areas, *chicharrón* is also added to the cornmeal dough of *arepas* and tamales. To this end, it is previously fried, well drained, and ground. Many South Americans enjoy eating it at breakfast.

The sausages of the *cocina criolla* deserve a section to themselves. Even though their preparation is based on the Iberian patterns in general, in South America they have been adapted in some ways. For example, in the eastern part of Venezuela, the *morcilla* (blood sausage) features large quantities of a small capsicum, known there as *ají dulce* (sweet pepper), which is not hot and provides food with a very special scent. Grated sugarloaf is also added to the blood, lending *morcillas* a very particular sweet flavor. By contrast, in Colombia, one of the most appreciated sausages is the *longaniza* (spicy sausage), which is a kind of long chorizo of some 20 cm (8 inches) that is not sweet at all, but rather salty.

Along the northern coast of Venezuela, as well as in some parts of Brazil and northern Peru, kid meat is used to prepare a wide range of very popular dishes. In Venezuela, these dishes are prepared with salted goat meat, which is known as *salón del chivo*. The cooking procedure includes desalting the meat and then stewing or frying it, always preparing the *sofrito*. Brazilians—who refer to this animal with two names, either *bode* (male) or *cabra* (female)—eat it roasted or stewed. And Peruvians use this animal to prepare a stew they call *seco de cabrito*, generally using the leg of the animal, which they season with salt, pepper, cumin, garlic, and hot pepper; then they add orange juice, brown the meat in oil, and add coriander and *chicha* to finish cooking.

The sheep taken to the Americas by the conquerors did not acclimatize to the warm regions, but rather to those with temperate or cold climates. Today, their meat is consumed especially in Peru, Brazil, Chile, and Argentina. In Argentina, a popular dish called *cordero patagónico* is very appreciated by gastronomes. In contemporary times, African sheep accustomed to the warm climate have been brought to Venezuela, for example. However, in Venezuela, lamb is not popular due to its somewhat rancid flavor. In the Andean countries, there is the *seco de cordero*, the cooking procedure of which is very similar to that of goat stew (*seco de cabrito*). In Brazil, people prepare a dish known as *buchada*, both with ram and with goat. The main ingredients of the dish are the head, entrails, intestines, legs, and blood of the animal, usually seasoned with coriander, chives, tomato, cumin, pepper, garlic, bay leaves, and vinegar. Typical-food recipe books recommend that these parts of the animal be extremely well washed before stewing. This Brazilian dish would be equivalent to the *mute de ovejo* prepared in western Venezuela, where it is also known as *mondongo de chivo* or *mondongo de carnero*.

Llama meat, along with that of alpaca, vicuña, and guanaco—frequently eaten during pre-Colombian times—are currently only consumed in some places, especially in the Andean rural areas. When offered in modern restaurants, they are appetizers. There is a dish, though, which is still consumed in Peru and Bolivia. It consists of a stew made with a tuber known as *olluco* (*Ullucus tuberosus*) in Peru, as *melluco* in Ecuador, and as *ruba* in Colombia, plus *charqui* (salted llama meat), hot pepper, cumin, pepper, parsley, and some stock, and is dyed with a yellowish color using a little annatto.

Hens have traditionally been the most appreciated domesticated birds, as their meat is considered to be of the highest quality and to provide the greatest sustenance. This is why they were preferred over chickens. Nevertheless, chickens are more consumed than hens nowadays, as they are less expensive. There are different ways of preparing hen depending on the zone within the South American continent. It can be roasted, stewed, used as a broth, or even fried. For example, in Peru, there is the famous dish *ají de gallina*, the preparation of which requires boiling a big, fat hen; removing the meat from the bones; shredding it; and adding it to a mixture of garlic, onions, pepper, different hot-pepper varieties, cumin, milk-soaked bread, and crumbled fresh cheese. This preparation is usually served with rice and is decorated with olives, hard-boiled eggs, lettuce, and parsley. It is a succulent dish that quickly sates anyone's appetite. In Brazil, hen is washed with lime juice; the meat is removed from the bones and seasoned with garlic and salt; it is put to cook in a pot where dry shrimp and peanuts have been previously sautéed in oil; stock is added—preferably from the animal—and it is cooked until the meat is tender; and at the end, some palm oil or *dendé* (as it is called in Brazil) is added. It is usually served with *farofa*, which is thick cassava flour. This succulent dish is called *xinxim de gallina*. Hen meat is also combined with rice or couscous, or used as a base for a pickling dish with vinegar, onions, carrots, bay leaves, and hot pepper. In Venezuela, the most famous hen-based dish is the *hervido*—a kind of broth, to which potatoes, cabbage, *arracacha*, and other Venezuelan tubers are added. A number of dishes are prepared specifically with chicken, such as *pebre* (a Catalan word meaning "pepper"), which consists of a chicken stew made with a lot of pepper. In Venezuela, this dish also features tomatoes, onions, garlic, olives, raisins, capers, cinnamon, and cloves; some sweet wine; and a little bit of grated brown sugarloaf. But there are many ways to prepare chicken: roasted, stewed, fried, or grilled. This latter form is very popular in almost all South American countries; many people go to specific restaurants where it is prepared as a specialty, not only to consume it there, but also for takeout. The Muscovy duck—native to South America and known there as *pato amazónico* (Amazonian duck)—is commonly found in farms in the rural areas and even in many cities of the region. It is either raised at home or purchased in the market. The Muscovy duck is a favorite delicacy throughout the continent, featuring a wide range of recipes depending on the country. For example, in Brazilian Amazonia, there is a famous dish known as *pato no tucupí*, which consists of a roasted duck previously marinated in salt, bay leaves, black pepper, cumin, and vinegar. Once roasted, it is cut into pieces and cooked in a juice from bitter cassava, to which garlic and an herb called *jambú* are added. It is served with cassava flour. It is a delicious dish for those who are accustomed to eating it, but a bit strange for those who have it for the first time. There is also the Peruvian dish *arroz con pato* (rice with duck), which is prepared with lots of chopped coriander. When more liquid than usual is added to this dish during cooking, it is called *aguadito de pato* (duck soup)—a recipe native to the Chiclayo zone.

Even though all South American countries have created laws to protect wild animals, especially those species that have traditionally been hunting targets, some people—mainly from rural areas—continue to hunt and poach, and obviously continue eating game meat. Among the most appreciated game meats are that of paca or *lapa*, which is either stewed or oven roasted, and that of armadillo or *tutu* (as it is called in Brazil), which is usually stewed. Another animal that is hunted, although today raised on farms (especially in Argentina), is the viscacha, which is pickled.

Fish

Both the coasts bordering practically the whole continent and the vast and complex network of rivers watering its interior offer a bounty to South American cuisine. Seafood and fish have been consumed since pre-Columbian times and are an extremely important source of nutrients for the population.

One of the most famous dishes from the Pacific Coast is said to be the *cebiche*, which is found up the coast even to Mexico. This fish should be very fresh and preferably of white meat. During pre-Columbian times, it was cut into pieces, marinated with hot pepper, and eaten raw. Then, with the arrival of the Europeans, it began to be marinated in lime juice from the lime tree they brought over, along with onions and coriander.

From the coasts of Ecuador to the north, preparing *cebiche* involves using tomatoes and sometimes orange juice and even oil, pepper, or garlic. The only condition for this food not to be detrimental to one's health is that it should be freshly taken from the sea, which also provides for a really delicious flavor. Thus, a genuine *cebiche* cannot be prepared if extremely fresh fish are unavailable. A mixed variety of *cebiche* includes not only fish, but also shrimp, lobster, mussels, and other sea products. Nowadays, other ingredients, like mushrooms and chicken, are also used to prepare it.

Cebiche de Pescado (Ecuador)

- 1 pound fillets of white-fleshed fish (very fresh)
- 1/2 cup lime juice
- 1 teaspoon salt
- 1 medium onion, cut into very thin, round slices
- 1 medium ripe tomato, peeled, seeded, and finely chopped
- 1 teaspoon parsley, chopped
- 1/2 medium red chili, finely chopped (or 1 teaspoon hot sauce)

Cut the fish fillets into 1 1/2-inch-long by 1/2-inch-wide strips. Place them in a bowl with the lime juice and salt. Set aside to marinate for 3 hours. Then add the onions, tomatoes, parsley, and the chili. Mix well and adjust seasoning. Serve cold. If desired, accompany with toasted bread and avocado slices. (4 servings)

In Peru, *cebiche* is usually served with corn kernels (*choclo*) and with sweet potato (*camote*). The fish is marinated in the lime juice for a very short period, compared to what is usually the case in Chile, where the fish is cut into strips and marinated a whole day with vinegar, white wine, onions, garlic, and aromatic herbs. It is in fact one of the most versatile dishes of South American cuisine, which probably accounts for its great success among both natives and foreigners.

Cebiche (Peru)

- 2 pounds red snapper
- 1/8 tablespoon Tabasco sauce
- 3/4 cup lime juice

- 1 tablespoon fresh cilantro, chopped
- 1/2 teaspoon salt
- 1 medium red onion, peeled and finely sliced
- 1 tablespoon red pepper, finely chopped
- 6 leaves iceberg lettuce
- 1 fresh medium hot pepper

Cut fish in 1-inch by 1/2-inch strips. Set aside in the fridge to marinate for 2 hours in lime juice, salt, and Tabasco sauce. Afterward, add chopped onions, hot pepper, and cilantro, and leave in the fridge for 1 hour more. Serve cold on a leaf of iceberg lettuce with round slices of onion on top. Accompany with crackers or toasted bread triangles. (6 servings)

If *cebiche* is the typical fish-based dish of the Pacific South American coast, fried fish is the typical one of the Atlantic coast, including the Caribbean one. Big fish is cut into round slices, while small fish is fried whole. Fish is fried in a lot of hot oil and, once drained, is simply served with lime slices, accompanied by the typical plain boiled rice. The Spanish-speaking South American countries inherited this technique from Andalusian cuisine. Sometimes, fried fish is marinated, along with some vegetables, such as onions and carrots (in round slices), green beans, bay leaves, and Jamaican pepper, in which case it is called *escabeche*. This is also an old Iberian dish, to which hot pepper is also added in some countries of the Andean zone, such as Peru. As for fish stews, it can be said that in the Caribbean coast, from Colombia, Venezuela, and the Guianas, fish is stewed in milk extracted from coconut pulp, while in Brazil this technique is also applied, not only for the preparation of fish, but also of shrimp, to which palm oil (*dendé*) is added—resulting in a dish called *muqueca*.

Muqueca Bahiana (Bahian Boiled Fish) (Brazil)

- 1/3 cup lime juice
- 2 green peppers, finely chopped
- 6 fillets (approximately 1 pound) white-fleshed fish
- 4 tomatoes, peeled, seeded, and chopped
- 1/2 cup olive oil
- 1 cup coconut milk, extracted from pulp
- 2 1/2 teaspoons salt
- 1 cup hot water

- 2 cloves garlic
- 2 tablespoons flour
- 3 large onions, finely chopped

Mix salt, two chopped onions, and lime juice in a bowl. Add the fish and set aside to marinate for about 2 hours. Pour the mixture in a saucepan. Add the tomatoes, the remaining onion, green peppers, and oil. Adjust salt and add 3/4 cup coconut milk. Cover the saucepan and cook over low heat for about 20 minutes. Remove the fish from the pan. Add the cup of water to the remaining sauce. Mix vigorously. Strain. In the remaining coconut milk, dissolve the flour and add to the sauce. Cook this over low heat, always stirring until it thickens. Make sure lumps do not form. Place the fish on a serving dish and pour the sauce over it. Serve with white rice. (6 servings)

Brazilians also prepare fish or shrimp in coconut (always using palm oil), but adding cassava—a dish that receives the name *vatapá*. To the south of the Andean region, in Chile, there is a famous dish called *congrio en fuente*, which is best prepared with red cusk-eel (*Genypterus chilensis*). This is a stew prepared in a clay dish or pot, using onions, tomatoes, hard-boiled eggs, toasted bread slices, parsley, hot pepper, salt, and pepper. Fish fillet pieces are intermingled with layers of the ingredients until the container is filled. A layer of toasted bread is put on top. It is then oven roasted, which results in a juicy fish.

In South America, a wide range of freshwater fish have successfully competed with the fish from the sea for time immemorial. In large rivers like the Orinoco, the Amazon, the Paraná, and the Paraguay, there are plenty of very tasty fish, which are thus very much sought after by the people either living by the rivers or far from them, but who are still very aware of their gastronomical value. One of the most coveted inhabitants of these waters is probably the one called *valentón* in Venezuela, *lau-lau* in the Guianas, *surubim* in Brazil, and *surubí* in Argentina. This fish has firm meat—as it is usually more than three feet long—and has a very good flavor. This gift from the rivers can be prepared in varied ways: grilled, fried, or stewed, and either without any seasoning or with varied sauces. In the Orinoco river basin, there is a famous fish known as *morocoto* (*Piaractus brachypomus*) with a flat body, a brownish-gray color that lightens toward the abdomen, and thick bones. Locals cut the fish in such a manner that they are able to take some sort of ribs out of it, which are generally fried after seasoning with garlic, lime, and some hot pepper. Another fish from the same region is the *pavón* (*Cichla orinocensis*), which can get over 60 cm (23 inches) long and reach up to 12 kilograms. It is of a yellowish color and has three dark spots running along its body, plus another one on its tail. It is not only found in the Orinoco river, but also in the Amazon basin. It is very much sought after due to the high quality of its meat, and, just like the *lau-lau*, it can be prepared in a number of ways. Many people prefer to grill it, which requires gutting.

Even though the South American region is endowed with a great variety of fish, its inhabitants decided to also breed some species brought from abroad, such as trout and salmon. Fish breeding has taken root in Venezuela, Peru, and Argentina. By the middle of the twentieth century, trout breeding was already carried out in Venezuela and Peru, even of the so-called *trucha salmonada* (salmon trout), which is larger than the common one. In Argentina, not only trout, but also salmon production has prospered. Salmon breeding in Chile must be highlighted, as it has brought about prosperity for many entrepreneurs, becoming one of the key export items of this country due to the size and quality of the specimens produced.

Vegetables

It is only natural that countless dishes have been invented in South America on the basis of vegetables native to the continent, such as potatoes, cassava, corn, beans, and palmettos. There is also rice, which—even

Xikrin Indian eats traditional food, Amazon, Brazil. © TRIP/ Ask Images.

though native to Asia—is perfectly acclimatized to many locations of the continent, becoming one of the staples for South Americans.

Among tubers, first and most important are the potatoes. These kinds of queens of the Andean cuisine are appreciated from north to south, not only as sides to other dishes, but also as independent preparations, as is the case of the *papas chorreadas* (from Colombia). The latter are prepared with medium potatoes, which are peeled and boiled in salted water until cooked; the water is drained and they are served on a plate. The potatoes are then covered—therefore their name, *chorreadas*—with a sauce made with grated cheese, tomatoes, onions, salt, cumin, and pepper.

Papas Chorreadas (Colombia)

- 12 medium potatoes
- 1 large onion, finely chopped
- 1 pound white cheese, grated
- 1/2 pound tomatoes, peeled, seeded, and finely cut
- 1 tablespoon salt
- 1/4 teaspoon ground cumin
- 1/4 teaspoon ground pepper

Thoroughly wash the potatoes. Peel them partially, leaving some skin on, and boil them. In a separate frying pan of medium depth, sauté the onions and tomatoes with the condiments in the oil until onions are translucent. Remove the mixture from heat and add the grated cheese, evenly mixing it. Serve the potatoes on a flat platter and cover them with the sauce just before serving. (6 servings)

The country with the widest range of potato-based recipes in the Andean zone is probably Peru. One of them is the *papas a la huancaína*, consisting of boiled potatoes that are cut into round slices; covered with a sauce made with hot peppers, fresh cheese, and oil; and then decorated with slices of hard-boiled eggs and black olives. Another dish is the *causa* (literally "cause")—a curious name for a dish consisting of mashed potatoes (prepared with hot pepper and cheese) bordering a chicken or tuna stew. In a similar dish, the *ocopa*, peanuts and shrimp are added to the mashed potatoes. There are many other Peruvian recipes, though, based on the use of this appreciated tuber.

As for the dishes prepared with cassava—rather typical of the Amazonian region—they involve peeling the tuber, cutting it into elongated pieces, and either frying or boiling them. The pulp is also used to prepare a pastry that is used in the preparation of empanadas (to be filled with cheese or meat) and also of *buñuelos*. In Colombia and Venezuela, the famous root *arracacha*—also known as *apio criollo*—is used to prepare *buñuelos* that, once fried, are covered with sugarloaf syrup scented with cloves.

Corn also plays a very important role and is used to prepare countless dishes ranging from the South American breads—the *arepas*, tamales, and *humitas*—to different types of pies, such as the *pastel de choclo* (very popular in Chile and Argentina), the polenta (the typical Venezuelan pie, made with tender corn and filled with stewed pork or chicken), and the *mazamorras* (prepared in the whole continent).

Pastel de Choclo (Chile)

Stuffing
- 2 pounds lean beef, chicken, rabbit, or pork
- 2 medium onions, peeled and finely sliced
- 3 tablespoons olive oil
- 1/2 tablespoon white pepper
- 1 tablespoon dry ground oregano
- 1 tablespoon cumin (in grain form)
- 1 tablespoon cooking salt
- 1 tablespoon ground paprika

Dough
- tender corn kernels from 12 ears of corn
- 5 tablespoons and 1 teaspoon unsalted butter
- 1 tablespoon cooking salt
- 1 tablespoon and 1 teaspoon sugar
- 1/8 teaspoon grated nutmeg
- 5 cups corn pulp, ground and drained

Additional Elements
- 3 hard-boiled eggs, sliced
- 8 black or Kalamata-style olives, pitted and sliced
- milk (have some close at hand in case it is necessary)

Stuffing. Boil the beef (or chicken, rabbit, or pork) for 1/4 hour. Then cut it into chunks of about 2 cm (1 inch). Preserve stock. Put the onion in a saucepan and cover it with oil. Add the meat and cook for 5 minutes. Add the spices and a ladleful of the stock. Adjust seasoning. Remove from heat and mix well.

Dough. Crush the corn kernels in a blender or dicer until well ground, adding a little milk if necessary. Place the obtained paste in an aluminum or Teflon saucepan. Add the butter, nutmeg, and salt. Cook over medium heat, always stirring to keep it from sticking. Remove from heat after 1/2 hour or when a thick paste has formed. Add the sugar and mix well. Spread a thin layer of the paste (*choclo*) in a deep serving dish, add the stuffing, place the hard-boiled egg slices and the sliced olives on top, and then cover with the remaining *choclo* paste. Bake in a preheated 350°F oven until the pie surface browns. (6 to 8 servings)

Also, corn kernels are used as an accompaniment to a number of stews or as an ingredient for the preparation of salads or even soups. One of the foods that is commonly consumed in the whole Andean region is corncobs, which are simply grilled or boiled in salted water. Then butter and salt are added and any other sauce is served with them. In South America, corncobs are considered a very popular snack, as they are commonly sold in public areas, such as squares, markets, and bus or railroad stations, especially by women, who generally offer a wooden stick too, which is used to spear them through one end. Moreover, a number of sweet dishes are based on cornmeal, some of them being the *majarete* (Venezuelan pudding made with cornmeal, milk extracted from coconut pulp, and sugar, then sprinkled with cinnamon) and the *mazamorra morada* (Peruvian pudding made with wine-purple corn kernels that when soaked produce a purple liquid that is thickened with cornstarch and sprinkled with cinnamon before serving).

In South America, beans are not only used to prepare soups, but also stews. They are first soaked for at least 24 hours and then cooked in some stock made with pieces of fresh pork or ham seasoned in very different ways, always using either small or large quantities of hot pepper and sometimes adding some sugarloaf. An example would be the well-known *feijoada*, typical of the Brazilian cuisine. Bean-based stews usually contain diced potatoes, as well as carrots, while some coconut milk from pulp is sometimes added to the broth, especially in the coastal areas.

Feijoada a la Brasilera (Brazil)

- 2 pounds fresh lean beef
- 1 pound jerky
- 1/2 pound smoked bacon
- 1/4 pound salty pork fat

- 1 pork sausage
- 1 medium clean beef tongue
- 6 cups water
- 10 slices orange
- 2 pounds black beans
- 10 teaspoons cassava flour or tapioca (natural or toasted)
- 2 pounds rice
- 1 tablespoon Tabasco sauce
- 2 tablespoons olive oil
- 1 large onion, finely chopped
- 1 clove garlic, finely chopped
- 1 bay leaf
- 1 tablespoon salt

Leave pork fat, jerky, and bacon to soak in water overnight. Drain the water the next morning. Sauté the onions, garlic, and bay leaf in the oil for about 15 to 20 minutes. Set aside. Place the beans in 6 cups of water. Add the salt and set to boil. As soon as the beans come to a boil, add the pork fat, sausage, jerky, fresh beef, tongue, and bacon. Then add the *sofrito* of onions, garlic, and bay leaf. Wait until it boils again and turn heat to low. Let cook for 6 hours. Then add the Tabasco sauce. Remove from heat when the meat is almost completely cooked. Cook the rice in water, adding additional salt to taste. To serve, place all the meat on a serving dish and the beans and rice in two other different dishes. Garnish the meat with the orange slices and tapioca. (10 servings)

Beans are also used to prepare purées, which are consumed as accompaniments to beef, poultry, and fish. Cod or any other salty fish is commonly eaten with beans, an example being the dish typical of the Venezuelan Caribbean coast known as *machucado*. Sometimes beans go with rice, as in the classic dish *arroz con frijoles negros* (rice with black beans), which is consumed throughout South America.

There are many rice-based dishes in the continent, ranging from the universal *arroz blanco criollo* (typical plain boiled rice), which is practically eaten every day in almost all South American households, to rice-based dishes prepared with coconut milk extracted from pulp, which are very popular in the Colombian coasts, particularly in the city of Cartagena. These are mainly savory dishes, although they many times contain raisins and some grated sugarloaf. There is also another dish found almost in the whole region, namely *arroz con pollo* (rice with chicken, probably of

Iberian origin), as well as *arroz con mariscos* (rice with shellfish, also of Iberian origin). Rice also plays a key role in desserts. The *arroz con coco* (rice with coconut), clearly a sweet dish, is known in the whole region, with the most distinguished version belonging to the Bahian cuisine of African influence. Another rice-based dessert that has to be mentioned is the *arroz con leche* (rice with milk), which is also the result of the Hispanic-Portuguese influence on South American cuisine. This dessert is loved by children and is prepared by convent nuns as well as housewives.

The tender young shoots (palmettos) of some palm trees of the New World have been playing a key role in South American cuisine, often replacing asparagus, which grows well in South American vegetable gardens but is still considered a foreign vegetable. Both the *ensalada de palmito* (palmetto salad) and the *palmito al gratén* (palmetto au gratin) are commonly prepared at home and in restaurants. Even though these vegetables were first only found in the Amazonian region, they are now found almost everywhere, as the food industry has included them in its range of canned foods. Palmettos from Venezuela, Brazil, Ecuador, and Peru are particularly preferred.

Desserts

Desserts are another essential category within the dinner menu, ranging from the great number of *frutas en almíbar* (fruits in syrup) to pastry and other egg-based desserts. Patties—usually a savory dish—are prepared for dessert in Chile, an example being the so-called *empanadas de crema.*

Empanadas de Crema (Chile)

Dough
- 2 cups wheat flour, sifted
- 2 egg yolks
- 2 tablespoons sugar
- 3/4 cup milk

Stuffing
- 1 cup wheat flour, sifted
- 2 cups milk
- 1 cup sugar (less the two tablespoons used for the dough)
- 1/4 pound butter (at room temperature)
- 5 egg yolks
- 1 teaspoon vanilla extract

- 1/8 teaspoon salt
- enough fat for deep-frying

Stuffing. Scald the milk in a pot and add the sugar and then the vanilla. Beat the egg yolks in a bowl. Add the flour little by little, mixing well, until a smooth mixture is obtained. Gradually add the mixture to the milk, always stirring. Pour everything in a pot and cook over low heat for about 5 to 6 minutes until a smooth and thick mixture has formed, always stirring. Add the butter and mix well. Remove from heat and let cool, covering the pot. Meanwhile, prepare the dough.

Dough. Place the sifted flour in a bowl. Add the egg yolks, sugar, and milk. Mix until a smooth dough is obtained. On a floured surface, roll out the dough with a rolling pin to a thickness of 1/8 inch. Cut the dough into rounds of about 4 inches in diameter by means of a dough or cookie cutter. Pour 1 tablespoonful stuffing onto each round. Fold over and carefully press with a fork to seal the edges together.

Final directions. Heat fat to 360°F. Carefully place the small patties, one by one, into the hot fat with a skimmer. Fry them for some 6 to 7 minutes until brown. Drain well and place them on a serving dish. Sprinkle them on both sides with sugar. Serve warm or cold.

As mentioned in chapter 2, cane sugar was introduced in South America by the Spanish and Portuguese, so it can be said that desserts appeared in the region as a result of their arrival. It was during the lengthy colonial times, and also during republican times, that the typical South American desserts came to life. They are featured today by domestic and restaurant menus along with other desserts from French, Italian, and U.S. cuisines, and even from other places like China.

Many fruits are prepared in syrup, as jelly, or in a glazed form, making up an extensive repertoire of typical desserts. Some are native, and others were brought by the Europeans. Such fruit-based desserts are typical all over South America. They differ from the ones prepared in Europe, as they are made with green (i.e., unripe) fruits and feature thick syrup, while the ones prepared in the Old World are made with ripe fruits and feature thin syrup. Some well-known examples are papaya, guava, cashew, pumpkin, figs, and mango in syrups. They are very sweet and not very much appreciated by foreigners. The ways to prepare them are considerably rooted in the Arab traditions that influenced the Iberian cuisine during the Middle Ages. When the fruit pulp is cooked for a long time, solid jellies result. Some fruits are also crystallized and served whole or in pieces. An example of these jellies are the ones made with guava called *bocadillos de guayaba*. The ones prepared in Colombia are very famous (particularly those from the city of Vélez), consisting of some 5 cm long by 2.5 cm wide (2 inch long by 1 inch wide) rectangular pieces of guava jelly that come wrapped in dry leaves from *bijao* (*Heliconia bihai* L.). This plant is found in the humid tropical forests of the New World. In the Guianas and Brazil, the fruit from the cashew tree (usually known for the nuts it produces) is crystallized to make a dessert. The Brazilian version is particularly famous. Nowadays, many of these syrups, jellies, and crystallized fruits can be found in the supermarket. However, according to traditionalists, these industrially processed sweet dishes have lost their original flavor, probably because of the use of preservative substances.

Egg-based desserts play a significant role in South America. Even though they have a Hispanic-Portuguese origin, some varieties taste different from the ones prepared in the Iberian Peninsula, as they are made with different ingredients. This is the case of crème caramels. They are prepared the Iberian way, but pineapple juice, pumpkin pulp, or coconut milk extracted from pulp is added, resulting in typical South American varieties. There is a dessert called *huevos chimbos*, which is prepared by beating egg yolks, cooking them in a double boiler (in either small or large containers), and then covering them with syrup made of rum or brandy to be soaked up. A similar dessert is prepared in Paraguay, which is called *huevos mollos*:

Huevos Mollos (Paraguay)

- 6 egg yolks
- 1 stick cinnamon
- 1 cup sugar
- 1 cup water
- 6 tablespoons hazelnuts and almonds, chopped

Beat the egg yolks until creamy and white. Pour them into a refractory glass dish of medium depth to a thickness of about 4 cm (1.5 inches). Steam for about 20 minutes. Let cool. Dice the mixture into 1-inch pieces. Over medium heat, make a syrup of water, sugar, and cinnamon. When it reaches a honey-like consistency, add the egg pieces and let boil until these absorb the liquid. Let cool and place on a serving dish. Sprinkle with chopped almonds and hazelnuts.

Another egg-based dessert is the so-called *bienmesabe*, typical in Venezuela, which is also based in the use of egg yolks, to which coconut milk extracted from pulp is added to make a cream. This cream is poured on top of pieces of sponge cake soaked in muscatel wine, which are finally sprinkled with ground cinnamon. There are also the *merengones*, which result from the beating of sweetened egg whites and their baking on a usually round tin that is then placed on a tray. Layers of the meringue are intermingled with layers of fruit such as soursop, cherimoya, loquat, mango, or strawberry and finally covered with whipped cream.

Another dessert subclass is cakes, of which there is also a wide range. Sponge cake layered with marmalade—made from guava or soursop, among other fruits—and *crème pâtissière*, with the whole cake covered by a kind of Italian meringue, plays a significant role. There are also the so-called *golfeados*, from Venezuela, which are made with sugarloaf syrup flavored with anise, very similar in shape to Danish pastries.

The South American confectionary field also features small sweets made of corn or wheat flour, as well as caramel, coconut, and other ingredients from the region. These sweets, mainly loved by children, are usually sold in stores known as *dulcerías* and are nowadays also industrially manufactured. Some of these are candied coconut, soursop, or milk; the *alfajores* (made in the whole Andean zone), which are floury cookies filled with a sweet milk preparation (*dulce de leche*).

Alfajores (Argentina)

- 1 1/2 cups cornstarch
- 1/2 cup wheat flour
- 1 teaspoon baking powder
- 1/3 pound butter (at room temperature)
- 1 cup sugar
- 1 egg
- 2 egg yolks
- 1 teaspoon vanilla
- 2 teaspoons lime rind, grated

Lightly cream the butter. Then, add sugar little by little while continuously beating until well mixed. Add the egg and egg yolks and continue beating until a smooth and foamy cream has formed. Add vanilla and grated lime rind. Sift together cornstarch, baking powder, and wheat flour; add to the butter cream; and mix well. Knead until the dough is smooth. Let it rest for 10 minutes. Preheat the oven at 325° F. On a lightly floured surface, roll out the dough with a rolling pin to a thickness of 1/3 inch. Cut the dough into rounds with a round cookie cutter or any other similar instrument (trying to obtain an even number) and place them on a buttered baking sheet. Bake for 20 minutes or until slightly brown. Remove from oven and let cool. Sandwich the cookies together with *dulce de leche* (sweet milk dessert). (makes 15 to 20 sandwich cookies)

Dulce de Leche (Argentina)

- 2 cans condensed milk
- enough water to cover the two cans placed in a pot

Set the water to boil over high heat in the pot, where the cans have been placed. Let simmer for 1 1/2 hours. Add hot water as needed to make sure that the cans are always covered by the liquid. Let them cool. If you want to accelerate cooling, carefully place the cans under running water. When the cans are completely cool, open them and fill the *alfajores* with the obtained *dulce de leche* using a spatula or a spoon. (8 to 10 servings)

Dulce de leche is a common dessert in all South American countries and can be prepared in different ways. There is the *dulce de leche cortado* (of lumpy consistency, seasoned with orange leaves), the spread used to fill the *alfajores*, as well as the solid variety.

5

Eating Out

Eating out is not a new habit in South America, as there have been food stands in the streets and markets since colonial times. Restaurants and cafés first appeared in the nineteenth century and took on special significance in the twentieth century. Fast food in the continent comprises not only hamburgers, hot dogs, and other similar foods, but also native dishes that can be considered to be fast foods. Industries and businesses usually have cafeterias, but it is also common for employees to bring food from home to the workplace in special containers, which can be considered a manifestation of an old habit of eating at home.

Most people who live in South American—mainly urban—populations are forced to eat out at least once a day, especially in big cities and at lunch time. This habit has been principally determined by urban sprawl, which has translated into an increase in the distances between the home and the workplace; the congestion of road traffic, signifying a considerable time investment in commuting; and the working hours imposed by public offices and private firms, which do not leave employees much time for lunch. There are certainly some places with lower population density where the traditional habit of going home to have lunch is still maintained, but this is the exception to the general rule owing to an acceleration of the everyday-life pace in the region. Sometimes people even have to eat breakfast out. This is often reduced to a cup of coffee and some kind of snack, usually a sandwich, as people must eat very quickly so as not to be late for work. Under these circumstances, the only meal that is actually consumed at home is dinner. People have breakfast and lunch in traditional or modern restaurants and usually look for a place that sells a meal for prices they can afford, as salaries are not very high.

TRADITIONAL PLACES

Street-Food Stands

Street food dates back to colonial times. There are different types of street-food options, ranging from peddlers who walk along the streets carrying containers of food that has already been prepared to small or medium-size stands, where certain dishes are prepared on demand. The urban landscape of most South American cities is characterized by the presence of these small-scale vendors offering their edible merchandise to the passersby, who are often in a hurry and only have a couple of minutes to stop and have an empanada, *arepa*, or a piece of grilled meat, which can be seasoned with a wide range of mild or hot sauces either directly provided by the vendor or added to the food by the client from the plastic sauce containers available. As a drink, they can quickly have coffee, soda, orange juice, or juice made from any other fruit. Hot dogs and hamburgers are very frequently sold in these types of food stands. Street-food vendors are provided with a street

Indians selling grilled potatoes and meat on the street, Juli, Peru. © TRIP/W. Jacobs.

stall (*ventorrillo*), a street stand (*kiosko*), a pushcart (*carrito*), or simply some movable tables that are arranged for the day. Even though in the different countries health inspectors are required to make sure that safe food is being served at these stands, the truth is that the stands have become real headaches from a legal point of view, as the vendors are too numerous, they can move from one place to another, and there is not enough personnel to carry out the sanitary inspections. Inadequate sanitary conditions are therefore sometimes tolerated, which of course threatens consumers' health. But people often have no other alternative but to eat at these food stands, which have thus proliferated to such an extent that the old rule stating that it is bad manners to eat on the street is now only observed by very few people. The type of food served varies depending on the zone. For example, in Peru, one will find *anticuchos* (i.e., skewered grilled chunks of beef heart seasoned with garlic, hot pepper, and some other flavoring agent) or fresh corncobs that are boiled, drained, and then spread with some condiment. In Venezuela, it is common to find *arepas* filled with fresh cheese or ground or shredded meat, or *cachapas*, which are a kind of round pancake 10 to 13 cm (about 5 inches) in diameter made with fresh corn and also eaten with fresh cheese. In Chile, one will find empanadas with a wide range of fillings. So the foods sold in the street stands will vary throughout the continent, featuring the typical national touch.

Within this street-food category, another example are the carts that are pushed to sell ice cream by the *heladeros* or *sorbeteiros*, who usually announce their merchandise by sounding bells or by playing a chime-like music through a loudspeaker, which quickly attracts the attention of youth and children. There are also the pushcarts that sell drinks—for example, those found in Venezuela, which sell rice *chicha*, sugar-cane juice, *cocadas* (sweet coconut drinks), or coconut milk. Nowadays, the people who drive these pushcarts usually wear a uniform consisting of a white hat and jacket. They are modern substitutes for the peddlers of the past who used to announce their tasty food through cries, sometimes in verse.

Market Stands

South American markets have traditionally been places where people can purchase not only the food ingredients they need for cooking, but also prepared foods. The prepared food are almost exclusively typical dishes, contrary to what is the case in street-food stands, which not only sell typical foods, but also snacks of foreign origin, such as hot dogs and hamburgers. The people who buy these prepared foods in the markets are

Street vendor selling corn on the
cob, Bogotá, Colombia. © TRIP/
Dave Saunders.

generally those who are there for the daily shopping, and thus constitute
a captive audience. Markets are picturesque places, where a great variety
of food is offered to the visitors. One can find, for example, the special
fruits of the region, many of them only available in such markets, as they
are only grown in small quantities and are not commonly found in supermarkets or other food stores. Other key products that can be found are
game meat, which would never be available elsewhere; certain traditional
preparations; cornmeal dough to make the typical dishes; and farmhouse
cheeses and sausages, as well as many other foods that are native to the
region. Foreigners seeking everyday food will find samples of the native
food culture. In the Andean zone there are great rural markets, where the
natives sell their farm produce and culinary work. These places feature the
widest range of products that are not available in the chain stores. They
have, for example, many tuber varieties that are impossible to find in the
city markets. Visitors can also buy handicrafts, such as containers, plates,
trays, cups, and other such items made of clay, wood, or straw.

CONTEMPORARY OPTIONS

Restaurants and Cafés

Restaurants and cafés, a concept from Europe, began in South America
during the nineteenth century but are currently found throughout the

continent, where they have become part of the South American heritage. Historians of the various countries of the region have stated a number of dates for the emergence of the first restaurants in the capital cities. They all agree that they were introduced in South America by the middle of the nineteenth century. In the beginning, most of these places were run by foreigners, and the dishes served were mainly typical of European cuisine. The important role of foreigners in the establishment of restaurants and cafés in South America is demonstrated by the fact that many of them continue to have foreign owners. Many entrepreneurs in this field are European, mainly Italian, Spanish, and Portuguese, and to a lesser extent French and German. A very important role is also played by Asians, the largest proportion perhaps being Chinese, followed by Japanese, whose restaurants have increased in number in the last decades, for example in countries like Venezuela, where they did not exist before. Worth mentioning are also the Arab restaurants—especially Syrian and Lebanese. Those from India, which play a significant role in the Guianas, are still relatively scarce and are considered exotic in the other South American countries.

However, most restaurants are now run by South Americans, many serving the typical dishes of the continental areas. Some very popular restaurants are the Colombian *sancocherías*, the Peruvian *picanterías*, the Brazilian *churrascarias*, and the Argentinean *parrilladas*. The most prestigious restaurants may be the French ones, even though those offering international cuisine play the main role among the finest restaurants in quantitative terms. Those specializing in French food still enjoy great popularity. Many of these restaurants are considered to be elite, which means that their clients are solely from the upper classes. Nevertheless, there are a great number of modest restaurants that more people can afford.

Cafés were introduced in South America before restaurants, as they had already been established by the early nineteenth century in the capitals of viceroyalties and captaincies general, in some cases serving as a meeting point for many pro-independent revolutionaries. The number of cafés started to increase with time, and nowadays they have been established in practically all South American cities and locations. In the 1990s cybercafes emerged as a result of the globalization process. In such cafés, people surf the Internet while drinking a *cafecito* and snacking on a *bocadillo*. There are still traditional cafés in some of the South American countries, many of which were founded in the late nineteenth century. They have become a kind of national monument, as is the case of Café Tortoni in Buenos Aires, but their main role is to serve as tourist attractions and no longer as the meeting point for literary and political circles or *peñas*, as they once did. It seems that French-style cafés have mostly taken root in Argentina and Chile, and the largest number of them are located here. In these places, there is always a coffee machine imported from Italy that produces beverages of high quality, due to the fact that a number of South American countries produce some of the best coffee varieties, as is the case of Brazil, Colombia, and Venezuela. One of the most picturesque features of these establishments is the nomenclature used for the different kinds of coffees that are served. In Venezuela, for example, one can order a *negro* (strong infusion), a *guayoyo* (milder infusion), a *marrón* (with a touch of milk), and a *con leche* (more milk than coffee). In Colombia, there is the *tinto* (equivalent to the Venezuelan *negro*), the *aguatinto* (equivalent to the Venezuelan *guayoyo*), the *pintado* (which corresponds to the Venezuelan *marrón*), plus a great number of names found in the different countries of the region. There is in fact a varied and complex coffee culture among South Americans.

Luncherías

In South America, there is a type of food and drink store, whose name derives from the English word *lunch*, that can be categorized as halfway between cafés and restaurants. In these places people can have breakfast or a light lunch. They serve coffee, fruit juices, sodas, and other alcohol-free beverages, and even ice cream, milk shakes, and some desserts. These *luncherías* (lunching spots) have relatively low prices and are therefore very much frequented by the masses. They usually include a bakery and confectionery section as well as delicatessen. These places are very informal; even though there are waiters and a menu, you cannot expect the same treatment and variety of dishes offered in restaurants. In Venezuela, they are sometimes also called *panaderías* (bakeries), as in this country there are practically no stores solely devoted to the expenditure of bread, while in Brazil they are known as *lanchonetes*.

Fast-Food Stands

Fast-food stands were established in South America in the second half of the twentieth century. At the end of the twentieth century, many of the transnational fast-food chains were almost everywhere in the continent. The proliferation of restaurants serving hamburgers, hot dogs, charcoal-grilled chicken, sandwiches, and other similar dishes took place in the cities, along with the expansion of franchise food stores. This trend has been one of the consequences of the rapid and intense urban-development process and the acceleration of everyday life. Mass production of this type of food has enabled the enterprises involved to offer tempting low prices that have attracted a large public, especially young people. Even though South Americans have not abandoned their connection to the traditional foods of their own countries, the time factor has driven them more and more toward the consumption of fast food. However, this movement has also featured native rivals, who have entered the market and competed with the foreign fast-food restaurants by offering typical dishes that fit into the pattern of this type of food. As an example, in Venezuela, the ancient corn bread called *arepa*—which can be mass-produced, filled with a wide range of preparations, and served as if it were a hamburger—has given rise to the so-called *areperas*. These restaurants emerged in the late twentieth century and have proliferated throughout the country. Stuffed *arepas* (*arepas rellenas*) can be consumed while standing. They are served on small cardboard plates and semiwrapped in paper napkins, so no cutlery is needed to eat them. They have the advantage over other fast foods of being a traditional dish and of allowing for a great variety of fillings, ranging from vegetables to beef, including cheese, scrambled eggs, chicken, fish, and countless stews. In these fast-food restaurants, the clients can choose from a number of different sauces to flavor the *arepa* according to their liking—not only mayonnaise, mustard, and ketchup, but also a wide variety of chili-based sauces, or milder ones made with coriander, avocado, or other ingredients. *Arepas rellenas* are offered at very competitive prices compared with those of foreign fast foods, which has resulted in their great success and will help them keep their place in the future.

At the Workplace

The increase in the number of companies and industries has in many cases led to the establishment of cafeterias on site for workers. These cafeterias usually offer balanced menus of fairly simple dishes, which can be consumed in a relatively short time and which the personnel can afford. These cafeterias are often under the supervision of nutritionists and strict health inspectors. But the food eaten in the workplaces where there are no cafeterias or dining halls can be considered an extension of domestic food, as workers bring homemade food to the workplace in lunch containers known as *vianderas* and *loncheras*, which are carefully prepared and filled at home. In these workplaces there is usually a special room with a couple of tables and chairs where people can sit and eat what they brought from home; or, in some cases, they simply eat the food inside their own offices. This option is obviously the less expensive one, and since the food containers are insulated to keep the food warm or cold, there is no need to reheat or cool. The lunch containers usually include a plate or bowl and even cutlery that can be washed or thrown out. The range of homemade preparations that are usually brought to work is fairly limited. It rather reflects the monotony that characterizes everyday domestic cuisine. The repertoire is usually limited to rice, chicken, plantains (fried or prepared in any other traditional way), pasta with tomato sauce and sometimes some ground beef, and other dishes of this kind. This simple lunch is generally accompanied with a soda or some store-bought fruit juice.

DINING OUT

If the various places where South Americans can go to eat are reduced to only two categories, namely "restaurants" and "other dining places," the latter would be the most frequented, simply because most people lack the money to be able to eat in restaurants. No matter how modest these restaurants are, they are outside the budget of most of the population, which incidentally confronts serious hunger problems. Nevertheless, when a celebration is in order, South Americans usually make an effort to celebrate by eating out at a restaurant—even if they have to depend on the contribution of those invited to the meal—as eating in a restaurant is considered synonymous with prestige. This is especially done for Mother's Day, Secretary's Day, birthdays, wedding anniversaries, and other special family events.

In general, restaurants are only frequented by people who are economically comfortable, and the ones that are top-rated have a further-reduced clientele. Although the restaurant industry has undergone significant development as a whole, South Americans have not abandoned their habit of eating at home. Deep down inside they—especially Chileans— probably prefer homemade food. However, in all South American countries a dining culture still enjoys certain validity despite the economic difficulties faced by the population. In almost every part of South American, but especially in the countries' capitals, there are gastronomic clubs or associations playing a considerable role in the food culture, as the few members belonging to them have significant purchasing power. Among the middle and upper classes there is a certain cult of gastronomy, which becomes evident in the publications devoted to this issue, as well as in the TV and radio programs and the festivals that often take place in restaurants and hotels of the different locations. These phenomena encourage people to eat out, as attractive, sometimes exotic offerings are made. From the 1980s on, a number of gastronomy academies have been established throughout the continent. There is the Argentinean Academy of Gastronomy, with headquarters in Buenos Aires; the Colombian Academy of Gastronomy, with headquarters in Bogotá; the Peruvian Academy of Gastronomy, with headquarters in Lima; and the Venezuelan Academy of Gastronomy, with headquarters in Caracas. These gastronomy associations have become centers that foster the development of the dining scene in the South American countries where they have been founded, especially in their capital cities, as their members usually organize dinners and other events to take place in the restaurants, and they have created awards that are given to both the establishments and the chefs.

There are also gastronomic guides that provide information on the main characteristics of the restaurants, sometimes classifying them according to certain criteria. These criteria are not homogeneous for the whole region yet, except for those used by the guide *América del Sur*, made with the support of the International Academy of Gastronomy and published in Barcelona, Spain, since the late 1990s. Most gastronomic guides do not give dining information for entire countries, but rather for their main cities, mostly the capitals. For example, in Venezuela, there is the *Guía Gastronómica de Caracas* by Miró Popic, first published in 1998; for the cities of São Paulo and Rio de Janeiro, there are restaurant guides by a group of authors published by Viana and Mosley and Vía Global, last published in 2004, as well as the *Guia Danusia Bárbara dos Restaurantes do Rio*, also with an updated version for 2004; for Buenos Aires, there are the *Guía de bares, cafés y restaurantes populares* (2003) by Gabriela Kogan and Gabriel Sánchez Sarondo, *Restaurantes de Buenos Aires 2003–2004* by Gabriel Fernández, which has been published for a couple of years, and *Restaurantes de Buenos Aires—Los Recomendados*, by Alicia Delgado and María E. Pérez. Apart from the printed guides, others can be accessed through the Internet, which are clear signs of the accelerated development that has taken place in the field of information on restaurants. At the same time, such publications are evidence of the diffusion and evolution of eating out in the continent.

6

Special Occasions

South Americans celebrate a great variety of special occasions in which food plays a main role. In some of them, people prepare special dishes that are only eaten on such occasions. These festivities take place throughout the whole year, the most important corresponding to the calendar of the Catholic religion—the one that has prevailed in the region for more than five centuries. By celebrating such old religious festivities every year, South Americans sort of revive the past. Many cultural elements of either Iberian or colonial origin are still alive—the latter being the traditions that came to life during the emergence of the South American *sociedad criolla*. Within this framework, the two most important celebrations are probably Easter and Christmas, but there are also other events of narrower scope such as the patronal festivals. Of special significance also are the celebrations based on the farming calendar, as agriculture has played a key role in South American societies until very recently. Even though most of the population now lives in cities, in the rural parts, people still celebrate certain dates that have been traditionally special within the sowing and harvesting context. Apart from the aforementioned festivals and religious festivities, a number of celebrations correspond to the different life stages, from childhood to old age—births, birthdays, weddings, and wakes.

It can be said that these celebrations break the monotony of everyday life, not only because special religious ceremonies are carried out, but also because of the parties and gastronomical preparations they are accompanied by. On the one hand, they constitute an occasion for experienced female cooks to prepare the traditional dishes or their latest specialties to impress the neighbors or the family. On the other hand, they make possible the reunion of friends and acquaintances, as well as the striking up of new friendships. So these celebrations promote and reinforce group membership within the community, religious, or familiar framework. On these occasions, people enjoy the food, dance, listen to the music, and perform generally traditional rituals, except at wakes. At wakes, people gather to comfort the deceased's family in their grief, although sometimes popular folk songs and music are performed.

South Americans have always celebrated a very large number of festivities throughout the year, some of which will be described below. These celebrations have resulted in a wealth of national public holidays that have suffered the consequences of modernization, as the governments of the region have decreed that many of these days would no longer have holiday status in the working sense, which of course has not been well received by the people.

RELIGIOUS FESTIVITIES

Most South Americans profess Catholicism. Even though people's religiousness is not homogeneous throughout the region, most South Americans show respect for the formal aspects and thus continue to celebrate holidays such as Easter and Christmas. As for the importance of food during these periods, fasting practices are still carried out, while certain special dishes are also prepared. There are also some festivities in which the Indian and African traditions are mixed with the Catholic ones. Some are considered heathen by the Catholics, such as the *candomblés* celebrated in Brazilian Bahia. A number of *ferias* are rooted in the Catholic traditions, such as the Velorio de la Cruz de Mayo, and celebrations taking place in many towns during patron-saint days.

Easter

The Holy Week (Semana Santa or Semana Mayor)—constitutes one of the so-called movable feasts, like Ascension Day and Pentecost, as it can fall earlier or later within the Church calendar. During this week, the holy mysteries of Jesus' Passion are commemorated, and no partying is allowed. According to the precepts of the Catholic Church, the faithful must refrain from eating meat during this week; they can consume vegetables and fish, except on Good Friday, when the fast has to be observed and thus no food is allowed at all. Because of the existence of such rules, special diets have been created for this period of the year. It is remarkable that in South America certain amphibious animals like the *chigüire* (capybara), *carpincho*, *baba* (a kind of small alligator), and terrapin have been included in the fish category since colonial times. Therefore, abstinence is not as strict in the region as it is, for example, in Europe. Special dishes are prepared for this specific occasion using not only sea and freshwater fish, but also the meat of the aforementioned animals.

In Venezuela, for instance, *chigüire* or *carpincho* meat is used in the Llanos to prepare a dish known as *pisillo*, while that of terrapins is used in the Orinoco-Amazon region to make a stew that is covered with beaten eggs, commonly known as *cuajado semanasantero*—its name derived from Semana Santa. In the coastal area, *escabeche de carite* is prepared for this week. This dish of Iberian origin is made with *carite* or mackerel (*Scomberomorus* spp.), a fish that abounds in the Caribbean Sea. In the Venezuelan Andean zone, there is a traditional meal known as *Siete potajes*, which is served as supper on Holy Thursday, generally including a soup of lentils, white beans, or chickpeas; sardines; a salad made of tuna, cod, or dried freshwater fish; rice with vegetables; cornmeal-bread rolls; plantain cake; and another dish that should not contain meat, all accompanied by *chicha* or *carato de arroz*.

In Colombia, there are a number of typical dishes prepared during Lent, such as *frijoles rojos con maduro* (beans cooked and ground with plantains, to which milk, pepper, cloves, and some brown sugarloaf are added); *locro* and *sopa de pandebono*, which are special dishes prepared for the days of abstinence (*locro* using potatoes, stock made with milk and water, beaten eggs, parsley, salt, and pepper, and *sopa de pandebono* using the same ingredients except the milk, and with stale bread and some coriander); and *taque*, an appetizer prepared with gourd, beets, carrots, cauliflower, and unripe peaches (cooked separately and then added) and seasoned with vinegar, oil, garlic, onions, chili, and parsley, making a mixture that is left to settle for eight days, after which the foam that has formed is removed from the mix. These dishes are mainly consumed in the Andean zone.

In Ecuador, the typical dish for Holy Thursday is *juanesca* or *fanesca*, a mixture based on the use of grains, legumes, milk, and cheese, to which dried fish is added. It also contains gourd or *zapallo*, beans, lentils, peas, *choclo* (fresh corn), rice, and, in some cases, slices of hard-boiled eggs. Another typical dish of Ecuador that is consumed on Palm Sunday is *chigüil*, which is a kind of tamale made with cornmeal, eggs, and cheese, wrapped in the corn husks and boiled in water. These preparations are also mainly eaten in the Andean zone.

In Peru, the dishes that are typically prepared for Lent are *sopa de olluco*, *mazamorras* (sweetened with brown sugarloaf or *chancaca* and scented with cinnamon), and a number of breads, among which aniseed bread and *rosquitas* are the most famous. In this period, Peruvians also eat dried fish stews made with cod (an imported product), *caballa del norte*, or *paiche*, obtained from the rivers of the forest. In Lima, some dishes that used to be prepared in the convents also became very famous, such as *ensalada cocida de Jueves Santo* or *ensalada antigua de Viernes Santo*. In southern Peru, people also prepare *chupe de zapallo* (gourd chowder) during Holy Week, which contains the *cuchuro* (algae of the Andean lagoons). In the Amazonian region, the typical dishes are *rumu-juane* and *paiche loretano a la vizcaína*. The former consists of dough prepared with cassava and fish and seasoned with onions, garlic, coriander, oregano, cumin, and pepper, which is then shaped into rolls that are wrapped in corn husks, tied with a string, and boiled in water. The latter is a stew made with the fish known as *paiche*, accompanied by white rice, fried or roasted plantains, and *chicha* or *guarapo*.

In Bolivia, specifically in the Andean region, people make a fish broth for Lent, which in the Aymaran language is called *challwa-wallakhes*. It is prepared with fish from Lake Titicaca or the nearby rivers. On Holy Thursday, in the capital city La Paz, Bolivians usually prepare a cod stew, and the desserts are *arroz con leche* (rice with milk) and fruit compotes. On Good Friday, they eat cod once again, but this time prepared *a la vizcaína*; *ají de khochayuyu* (marine algae imported from Peru); and, as dessert, *arroz con leche* or a sweet dish they prepare in the form of patties. It is particularly curious that cod-based dishes are prepared during Easter on the Andean highlands when there are other types of fish available in the lagoons and rivers of the zone; in any case, this is more evidence of the strong influence Spanish cuisine had on the region, which has lasted for centuries.

In Paraguay, people prepare a kind of soup for Lent known as *locro de Cuaresma* (Lent stew), which is based on the use of corn and seasoned with plenty of onions and tomatoes; whole eggs and fresh shredded cheese are also added to it. Milk can be also added, in which case the soup receives the name *locro blanco* (white stew). There is an ancient recipe used in Paraguay for this time period, namely *empanadas de Vigilia* (abstinence patties), with dough made with wheat flour, egg yolks, and some beef fat. The dough is kneaded a couple of times to obtain a sort of puff pastry, which is then filled with a fish stew containing chopped hard-boiled eggs, olives, and raisins, in addition to *sofrito*.

In Brazil, cod is consumed in all households of São Paulo and Rio de Janeiro during this time period. There is also the *ensalada de mayonesa*—similar to the Russian salad—which is also prepared on this occasion. People eat chocolate Easter eggs and also buy them in stores and give them as gifts to other people. The latter gift giving is a consequence of the Central European immigration. In Espírito Santo, on the Atlantic coast of Brazil, between Bahia and Rio de Janeiro, the *torta capixaba* is very famous, as it is the classic dish prepared for the abstinence period. It consists of a cake made with fish, shellfish, coconut milk from pulp, palmetto, olives, cloves, cinnamon, vinegar, and beaten eggs, the eggs serving as the cake's topping.

In Argentina, the classic dish for Lent is *chupe de leche,* which is a soup prepared without meat. For Easter Saturday and Sunday, Argentineans prepare *pastel de pollo*—a pie with dough made with cornmeal mixed with wheat flour plus eggs, salt, and milk, the filling consisting of chicken stewed with salt, bay leaves, onions, and oregano. In northern Argentina, people eat *yopará misionero*, which is a kind of stew made with corn, beans, onions, carrots, and gourd and seasoned with oregano and salt.

In Chile, people basically consume fish during Easter, especially cusk-eel, salmon, drumfish, and *reineta* (*Brama australis*)—the latter being somewhat similar to sole. The cooking method ranges from oven roasting to grilling, but they can also be used to make soups. Shellfish is also very much consumed in Argentina, especially clams (*machas*). Besides, a wide variety of pies are prepared with vegetables, such as Swiss chard, artichokes, or spinach.

Christmas

If Easter is characterized by fasting and the commemoration of Jesus' Passion, Christmas is a time for joy, as people commemorate Jesus' birth. The parties at Christmas are typically celebrated with the family, usually in the head of the family's house. Of course, it is also a time when special dishes are consumed. For example, in Venezuela, people prepare the typical national tamale, the so-called *hallaca*, generally accompanied by *jamón planchado*—cooked ham glazed with sugarloaf and often garnished with pineapple slices and cloves. Another typical Venezuelan Christmas dish is stuffed and roasted turkey, garnished with glacé cherries.

In Ecuador, the typical dishes prepared for Christmastime are *buñue-los*—fritters made with cornmeal, lard, salt, and eggs, and then covered with *chancaca* (sugarloaf) syrup—and *pristinos*, which are pieces of wheat-flour dough cut into stars, spread with beaten eggs, fried, and covered with sugarloaf syrup before serving. The typical Christmas beverage is *chicha de jora*—a sour corn-based drink.

There are certain similarities between the Christmas customs in South America and those of the Iberian culture. For example, in both, people put up a Nativity scene (in Spanish, *pesebre* or *nacimiento*)—a representation of Jesus' birth. Another typical custom of this time of the year are the *villancicos* (Christmas carols), also called *aguinaldos* in Venezuela and Colombia. These are songs about Jesus' birth, which are sung by the neighbors, who often play the typical instruments of the region as accompaniment to the songs. In Venezuela and Colombia, for instance, people play *cuatro*, *maracas*, harp, and *furruco*. The lyrics of these carols sometimes include the names of the typical foods the singers or *aguinalderos* request as they sing walking along the street during the festivities. For example, in Venezuela it is common to see such groups, many times spontaneously gathered on the street, improvising the verses to Christmas folk carols, like the following:

Greetings	**Saludos**
Here are we all,	Aquí estamos todos,
The very early risers,	Los madrugadores,
Singing Christmas carols	Cantando aguinaldos
Like nightingales.	Como ruiseñores.
Open the door, please,	Ábrannos la puerta,
We'd like to come in;	Queremos entrar;
Let us take a seat	Bríndennos asiento
And rest a little bit.	Para descansar.
We've sung the entire journey	Venimos cantando
Since we left Yaracuy;	Desde el Yaracuy
We've been eating *hallacas*	Hallacas comiendo
And drinking *cocuy*.	Bebiendo cocuy.

Requests	**Peticiones**
Here are we travelers,	Somos caminantes,
We don't ask for much;	Pedimos poquito;
Give us very little	Dennos por la Gracia
By the grace of God.	De Jesús chiquito.
Give me a Christmas treat,	Déme mi aguinaldo,

It could be some coffee;	Aunque sea café;
If it's still unripe	Si lo tiene verde
I would myself roast it.	Yo lo tostaré.
If you give us pastries,	Si nos dan pasteles,
Make them nice and warm;	Dénoslos calientes;
'Cause people can die	Que pasteles fríos
From eating them cold.	Matan a la gente.
We don't ask for wine,	No queremos vino,
And neither for rum;	Ni tampoco ron;
As your hospitality	Bástanos señores
Is good enough for us.	La buena intención.

In the other South American countries, people recite similar folk songs in the days before December 24, when a special dinner is usually served after midnight. This meal features dishes of varied degrees of elaboration, and some of them are only prepared during this time of year. On Christmas Eve, South Americans also attend the midnight mass known as Misa de Gallo before getting together to have the meal. In Colombia and Venezuela, the typical dishes prepared for Christmas Eve are *hallacas* or tamales. Colombians also prepare a pie with rice that is first soaked in vinegar and to which bacon, spareribs, and chicken are then added; another typical Christmas dish in Colombia is either *pernil al horno* (oven-roasted pork leg) or *lechón asado* (barbecued suckling pig), the typical Christmas desserts being *natillas* and *buñuelos,* the latter mostly prepared with *arracacha.*

In Peru, people make the popular South American turkey, which is accompanied by roasted or mashed potatoes as well as by string beans and carrots lightly fried in butter (in Lima) or green corn tamales (in Chachapoyas, Amazon region). In the coastal city of Lambayeque, there is a famous dish known as *empanadas de viento.* These are patties filled with meat that puff up when fried, then are drained and sprinkled with sugar. In the city of Puno, grilled meat is served with bread rolls called *quispiños,* which are made with cornmeal, wheat, or quinoa flour. Ram and chicken can also be prepared for Christmas Eve in Peru.

In Bolivia, the Christmas dinner is characterized by a dish known as *picana de Navidad,* which is a pot or stew made with lamb, beef, hen, carrots, turnips, onions, tomatoes, raisins, prunes, potatoes, fresh corncobs, and other ingredients; it is seasoned with black pepper, cloves, bay leaves, cumin, and oregano, plus some red wine. *Buñuelos de Navidad* are also typical of this country at Christmas. They are made with wheat flour, aniseeds, salt, sugar, and yeast, and sometimes also chocolate.

In Brazil, the typical Christmas dish is *cuscuz à Paulista*, which is based on corn and cassava flours, palmetto, shrimp, sardines, hard-boiled eggs, tomatoes, and several spices as condiments; another one is *feijoada do peru*, which is simply stewed beans with turkey bones—*peru* being the Brazilian name for this bird. As roast turkey is prepared for the dinner of Christmas Eve, the bones are kept—what Brazilians call *enterro dos ossos* (the burying of the bones)—and then used on New Year's Eve to prepare the *feijoada*. In almost all South American countries, the preparation of turkey has become a habit. It is usually oven roasted and stuffed in different ways according to the customs of each place. This is also the case of ham, which is cooked for Christmas by boiling it, glazing it, and finally garnishing it with round pineapple slices and glacé cherries.

In Paraguay, people prepare *sopa paraguaya* and *chipá guasú* during Christmastime, the latter being a kind of oven-roasted pie made with cheese and grated fresh corn. In Uruguay, a great variety of cold meat, cheeses, and roasted lamb or pork are consumed in December. In Chile, stuffed turkey or chicken is the typical mainstay of Christmas meals. In Argentina, people prepare chicken or turkey, grilled meat, and ice creams, and also enjoy nougats and *panettones*, the latter inherited from the Italian migrations. In these southern countries December, and therefore Christmastime, falls at the height of summer, so dinners are usually lighter, with cold meat playing a key role.

The dominant features of the South American dinner of Christmas Eve (Noche Buena) are the happy musical environment and the sumptuous meal served, as well as the exchange of gifts. By dinnertime—midnight—the children of the family should be sleeping, as this is the moment when their parents put their Christmas gifts in their bedrooms, as if they had been brought by baby Jesus.

Other Religious Celebrations

There are other days in the Catholic calendar when parties and special commemorations are also carried out. Examples of this are All Souls' Day and All Saints' Day, which fall on the first two days of November and when more parishioners than usual go to church and to cemeteries. These are occasions to present flower and food offerings. Bread and sweet dishes, shaped like humans or animals, play a key role. In Peru, for instance, people prepare the so-called *wawas*, which are bread rolls and biscuits in the shape of children for the festivities of November 1 (All Saints' Day). These sweet figures depict faces with all their features, made with caramel or wheat-flour dough and sometimes fondant. The rolls are dressed with clothes made of fabric or crepe paper. On All Souls' Day, Peruvian farmers visit the deceased in the cemeteries and bring them not only flowers and candles, but also *chicha*, spirits, fruits, and some food that they particularly liked when they were alive.

In Andean Bolivia, there is the tradition of preparing a special dish for the first two days of November to celebrate All Saints' Day and All Souls' Day: *uchu de Todos los Santos* (i.e., All Saints' chili). This dish is made with beef tongue, hen, red chili pepper, and guinea pig (one for two people) and seasoned with onions, garlic, cumin, and parsley; potatoes and hard-boiled eggs are also added, and the mixture is thickened with potato flour (*chuño*). This dish is accompanied by corn *chicha*. In the region of La Paz, during those same days farmers usually eat the so-called *humitas*, covered with *wiru* honey that is extracted from the canes of the corn plant. In Chile, both in Arica and in Antofagasta, there is an Aymaran tradition of widows going to the cemeteries on November 1 to celebrate All Souls' Day with a meal at the tombs of their dead husbands. They bring quinoa tortillas, *choclos*, patties filled with llama meat, and varied sweet dishes.

Other religious festivities correspond to the patron saints of churches, cities, or entire provinces. On these occasions, people perform religious rituals. Of particular significance are processions, in which the statues of the saints being honored are taken out of the church and paraded through the streets while people pray and sing along. But people also celebrate these days with music and food, the latter generally consisting of typical local dishes, which can be bought from peddlers on the street and also prepared at home. On the celebration of the day of Saint Anne (July 26) in Chuquisaca, Bolivia, ground corn tamales containing pork, chopped hard-boiled eggs, olives, and chili are prepared and served. On the day of Saint Clare of Assisi (August 12), patties filled with hen meat or cheese are sold on the street of this same locality, usually around the convent of the order of St. Clare. On Saint Anthony's Day (June 13) in Brazil, and especially in Rio de Janeiro, people usually buy a bag of blessed bread buns to take home when they exit the Saint Anthony's convent, as this is believed to bring an abundance of food to households. This day signals the beginning of the so-called Festas Juninas (June Feasts), as other saint days are also celebrated in June, namely Saint John's Day (June 24) and Saint Peter's Day (June 28). In the latter, people typically eat *pamonhas*, unripe corn soup, sweet rice, sweet potato cake, and two pies or *bolos* called *bolo de São João* and *bolo de Santo Antonio*, among other dishes.

South Americans also celebrate other religious festivities, resulting from the incorporation of beliefs and ceremonies of the pre-Hispanic peoples and of the Africans who were taken to the New World as slaves. Certain days that are apparently part of the Catholic calendar are actually reminiscent of ancient cults instead. Even though there are examples of these types of ceremonies in the Andean zone, where the proportion of indigenous people continues to be larger than that of other ethnic groups—as is the case of Colombia, Ecuador, Peru, Bolivia, Paraguay, and Chile—the most renowned ceremonies worldwide are those particularly influenced by the African traditions, considerably present in Brazil. An example is *candomblé*, which can be considered an African-Brazilian religion rooted in the religious practices of the African Bantu and Yoruba ethnic groups, which contributed large numbers of slaves to Brazil, especially to the region of Bahia. The presence of rites from this religion seems to have taken on special significance since the eighteenth century. Despite the efforts of the Catholic Church to extirpate such rites by constantly persecuting their manifestations, the rituals managed to survive until the present and are nowadays openly practiced. To this end, societies or brotherhoods were created, as well as their own male and female deities, initiation rites, and a number of other ceremonies to be celebrated throughout the year. These practices are carried out on special sites, namely the *terreiros de candomblé*, and are accompanied by food, which is considered a ritual symbol of force. Food creates communication ties among humans, gods, ancestors, and nature, as it is what activates the *axé*—the life energy or force. A number of ingredients and combinations are associated with certain meanings and are known as *cardápios votivos* (votive food). They are basically animals like cocks and hens, and also beans, corn, onions, shrimp, *dendé* oil, honey, cane and *cachaza* molasses, and cane spirits. Among the ceremonies in which foods are served and consumed, some of the most important are the *ossé* (celebrated every week), in which women offer votive foods to the *orixás* (as they call their saints); the *obori* (giving food to the head), which is an initiation ceremony in pursuit of health; and the *ajeum*, which is a party where people drink and eat the food of the gods in public. The most important ceremonies are those in which foods are offered to the *orixás*. These foods are called *ebó*, which means "present" or "gift." The *orixás* are known to each have particular food preferences. For example, Xangó prefers *carurú* leaves (the name given to a number of plants from the *Amarantaceae* family), corn and cassava flours, and mashed potatoes, while Exú, Ogún, and Oxóssi prefer *cachaza* (a type of rum)—often replaced by gin—and so on.

Another good example of the manifestations of Afro-Brazilian cults is the festival of São Cosme e São Damião, which is celebrated in Bahia on September 27—the so-called Día de Ibeji—in honor of these two saints, whose names are those of some twin saints, members of the *candomblé* calendar of saints' feast days. This day is commemorated by both Catholics and non-Catholics. The two saints are deemed to be protectors against illness as well as matchmakers. They are also said to bring good luck and to help find lost objects and realize unfulfilled ambitions. The main course served on this occasion is *caruru*. This time the word refers to a stew prepared with fresh dried shrimp; okra—in Brazil called *quiabo* (*Hibiscus esculentus*); lime; *dendé* oil; and peanuts. Other dishes that are typical of this day are *frigideiras* (fried snacks) and *efó*—a stew made of roasted peanuts and cashew nuts, leaves of *língua de vaca* (*Portulaca racemosa*), milk extracted from coconut, *dendé* oil, salt, and *malagueta* pepper. Once the saints are offered their food, the banquet continues until midnight. First of all, food is served to seven children; after they have gorged themselves, the adults start eating. As children also take part in these banquets, those from underprivileged households usually go door to door in the days before the celebration begging for money permitting them to have their own *caruru*. Some families welcome the passing-by children into their houses, inviting them to share this special stew.

COMMUNAL FESTIVITIES

South Americans also have a number of festivities that are not of a religious nature—for example, when the neighbors help with a house raising for which they receive no money. Such activities are generally related to the construction of houses or key dates within the agricultural cycle. They date back in some cases to pre-Hispanic times, but are still carried out today. This feast, in which the typical dishes and beverages of the region and locality are served, is called different names depending on the country. In Venezuela, it is called *cayapa*; in Colombia, Ecuador, Peru, Bolivia, Chile, and Argentina, it is known as *minga* (derived from the Quechua word *minkai*, which means "help at work").

As for the nonreligious festivities related to the agricultural cycle, some examples are the celebrations carried out on the occasion of the sowing or harvesting of the most important South American products, such as corn and potatoes. Within this framework, farmworkers usually gather in the same field during the work breaks to have a meal made of dishes they themselves bring. To give an example, in the Chilean localities of Arica and Antofagasta, people celebrate the feast of the potato—called Pachal-lampi by Aymaran farmers—at the end of October. People pair up to sow the tuber: the men open the holes, and the women throw the seeds in and cover them with the same earth. While performing these tasks, the people sing, and then, at noon, they have lunch of tamales filled with llama meat or pork, cooked *choclos,* and quinoa-based *poleadas* (a type of porridge)—everything very often seasoned with lots of hot pepper. Some-times, a single dish called *guatia* is prepared, which would be something similar to the Peruvian *pachamanca.* This meal is accompanied by a kind of spirit containing a high proof of alcohol, which is known as *patisunka.*

Particularly important are the festivities celebrated on the occasion of grape harvesting, which are typical of Argentina and Chile, as these are the most important South American wine-producing countries. This cel-ebration is deeply rooted, and its origins are obviously related to similar customs from the Iberian Peninsula. Yet in recent times grape harvests have become highly institutionalized and have been the subject of gov-ernmental decrees. In Argentina, the most famous grape-harvest feasts are the ones celebrated in February in the Mendoza Province. This event has become particularly well known with time, as it takes place in a great number of localities, and also because of the fireworks, the costumes of the participants, the dances, the music, the contests to choose the grape-harvest queen, and more. There is also a religious element represented in the blessing of the fruit and the worship of Virgin Mary, among others. In these festivities the main role is obviously played by wine, the activity of choice being wine tasting. To this end, a great exhibition of wines is orga-nized every March, in which the main wine producers take part; courses are offered to teach people how to taste wines, along with conferences on enology topics.

Chile also plays a very important role in wine production—an even more important role than Argentina, according to some. The Chilean grape harvesting is celebrated in March, sometimes also in the first days of April. These feasts are known worldwide, featuring a high level of orga-nization and efficiency. Particularly special are those in Santa Cruz (Col-chagua Valley), Curicó (Maule region) and Maipo (southern part of the Metropolitan region). In these feasts, people not only taste wines, but also culinary specialties from the region where they take place and from inter-national cuisine. Other South American countries also produce wine, but on a much smaller scale than Argentina and Chile, and even though they also organize such grape-harvest feasts, these cannot be compared to the Argentinean and Chilean ones.

As for the feasts organized around livestock work, especially that of herding the cattle together in order to brand them with different symbols corresponding to the different owners, Venezuelan cattle herders (*llaneros*) and those from Brazil, Uruguay, and Argentina (gauchos) usually take one animal and roast it at the end of the day when they have finished this hard labor.

PRIVATE PARTIES

Apart from the family parties celebrated during Christmastime, a number of important celebrations correspond to the different life stages. Births, children's birthdays, weddings, and wakes mark the transitions among the most important life stages. On these occasions, food plays a key role. They are featured by a clear predominance of the Iberian cultural influence, as well as by manifestations of the Catholic religion.

The christening of a newborn is deemed to symbolize the entering of the new person into the religious community, which is mainly Catholic in South America. The parents and relatives go to the church, where the priest gives the baby a name by means of certain prescribed rites, welcoming the child to the parish community. The fact that this person enters the Christian life is a cause for joy and, therefore, for a family party, in which people eat, but also drink a lot, as they toast the prosperity of the newborn. Even though there is no doubt that, formally, the most important person in the celebration is the baby who has been baptized, in reality, those who enjoy the party are the other children, and especially the adults. These parties are usually in the morning, with a special breakfast that includes cakes, cocoa, and coffee, as well as wines and other alcoholic drinks. They can also be held at noon, in which case a sumptuous lunch is served. There is a custom of distributing to all the guests a small printed or handwritten card with the name of the baby and the date on which the christening took place. Sometimes this card is accompanied by a small gift consisting of a couple of candies, such as almonds glazed with sugar in different (usually light) colors, generally blue if it is a boy and pink if it is a girl.

A birthday is also a reason to be happy and celebrate, especially in the case of children and teenagers, though adults also organize parties to celebrate their birthdays sometimes. In children's birthday parties, an afternoon snack (*merienda*) is usually served to all the children that have been invited. In some countries, such as Venezuela and Colombia, these parties also include a piñata, which is a large papier-mâché container filled with candies and small toys that is hung by a string from a hook in the ceiling or a tree by means of a pulley system, so that it can be raised and lowered by the adults. The children take turns being blindfolded and hitting the piñata with a stick they are given. After many missed hits, they eventually break the piñata, and the contents fall to the ground. This is the moment when all the children frantically scramble to collect as many goodies as possible. After the piñata ritual, a table is set with a birthday cake in the middle featuring the number of candles that correspond to the age of the birthday boy or girl. The candles are lit and everybody starts singing the typical birthday songs to the child, who must blow hard to blow out the candles. Next to the cake different desserts are placed, such as dishes in syrup, crème caramels, or *merengones*.

A wedding is another important milestone and is therefore celebrated with a big party, which would be more or less sumptuous depending on the economic status of the bride's and bridegroom's parents. Even though sometimes people celebrate their wedding in the morning hours, this ceremony is usually set for the early evening hours. After the religious ceremony, the guests accompany the bride and bridegroom to a place where a banquet is offered along with plenty of wine and other alcoholic drinks. The most important dish is the wedding cake, in which the confectioner has placed a ring or other small gift tied to a ribbon that emerges from inside the cake, along with other ribbons. According to the custom, all the bridesmaids take one ribbon each and pull them out at the same time; the one who gets the surprise will be applauded, as she is considered to be the next one who will get married. Music and dancing are also featured in these types of events. In the city, they usually take place in clubs or hotels.

In the rural areas, though, celebrations are more modest. Although there is also dancing, music, and food, the parties are less sophisticated. There are also other types of weddings, such as the ones celebrated by the indigenous peoples. An example is that of the Quechua and Aymaran farmers. In Chuquisaca, Bolivia, the Quechua prepare a ceremonial meal on special occasions, such as weddings. This meal includes what is known as *el blanco* (a peanut soup based on a stock made with chicken or with the back of the lamb), *picante de pollo con papas, pelachi uchu* (a Quechua expression meaning "peeled corn stewed with hot pepper"), *ají colorado, charqui,* and *papita menuda*. This meal is served to the most important people, as those who had not been directly invited to the party are simply given *mote de maíz pelado* (peeled boiled corn) or *cantu uchu* (a dish based in the use of hot pepper) in a calabash vessel. These dishes are followed by pastries: ring-shaped pastries, patties, biscuits, and cakes. As for the Aymaran peoples, those living in the city of La Paz, Bolivia, and its surroundings, usually offer up a special dish, the *wawa*, to the newlyweds when the religious ceremony in the chapel has come to an end and the newlyweds are already on the way home. This is a quinoa-based dish that is accompanied by fritters. At home, the newlyweds attend a ceremony consisting of the slaughter of two sheep, one male and one female, which are placed on the floor of the house before they are killed, one in front of the other, symbolizing the marriage. The guests are offered fritters, *k'ispiña*—small steam-cooked bread rolls made with peeled corn, cinnamon, aniseed, and lard—and *chicha* or alcohol to drink. All the guests must enter the party in pairs, each person carrying a gift, which usually consists of an *ahogado* (lamb-based soup with onions, *charqui*, and poached eggs) in the case of women, and fritters and *k'ispiña* or any fruit or beans in the case of men. The guests offering up this meal give it to the maid of honor and the best man, who pour the food into pots, from which it will be then served to the newlyweds and the other guests.

South Americans get together to pray and celebrate other religious ceremonies, as well as to offer condolences to the family of the deceased in the case of a death. As there is the custom of holding a wake, and since many people usually attend this event, snacks are served along with coffee, cocoa, or sodas to keep people awake throughout the night and the next morning before going to the cemetery for the burial. Although today wakes can be held at funeral parlors, some families prefer that the wakes be held at home. By tradition, when the deceased is a child, these funereal ceremonies are particularly special in a number of places of the continent. The ceremony is called *velorio de angelito* (little angel's wake), and it is a very old tradition that has been maintained for centuries. In these wakes, the small corpse is boiled before being placed inside the coffin, in order to preserve it for a longer period. There is music, folk songs regarding the deceased or the childhood that was interrupted by death, and dances, and of course food and drinks.

7

Diet and Health

Diet and health play significant roles in the South American food culture. Hippocratic-Galenic traditions are still preserved, along with the botanical-medicinal heritage of Indians and Africans, especially in rural areas. The ever-intensifying urbanization and the consequent increase in the number of professionals in the field of nutritional sciences, together with the quantitative and qualitative development of communication networks, have brought about partial changes in the traditional knowledge. A key issue of concern has been people's caloric requirements in the tropical lands and the nutritional values of staple foods. In modern times, a considerable number of citizens are facing nutritional deficiencies because of the poor economic situation, which has caused certain forced changes in their diets.

NUTRITIONAL LORE AND SCIENCE

Hippocratic-Galenic Traditions

The first to systematize knowledge on the art of healing people of their illnesses were the ancient Greeks, the most efficient and best-spread ideas being those of Hippocrates and, a long time afterward, Galen. Diet played a very important role in the treatises produced by these ancient physicians, containing precepts that have remained valid throughout the centuries. By the time of the European contact in South America, these precepts were still part of the cultural knowledge of physicians at that time. Some of these precepts are worth highlighting—for example, the differentiation between cold and hot foods, the need to prescribe special diets to sick people, and the advisability of detoxifications to cleanse harmful substances from the body, as well as other specifications on nutrition. They also wrote medicinal-plant repertoires, which were known as "medicinal material." The most famous book on this issue was the one written by Andrés Laguna and published in Antwerp in 1555 under the title *Pedacio Dioscórides Anazarbeo, acerca de la materia medicinal y de los venenos mortíferos*, which is a translation into Spanish with comments and notes on the book *Medicinal Material* written by the Greek physician Dioscórides, who lived in the first century B.C. This work—published several times during the sixteenth century—was brought to South America in colonial times.

The conquerors and then the colonists traveling from the Iberian Peninsula to the Americas brought with them this knowledge, and also many of the plants that were deemed to have healing qualities. Yet they also undertook the task of trying to classify the plants they found in the New World based on the patterns they had already learned in Europe. By the time the Europeans arrived in South America, the ancient Greek concepts were no longer limited to the physicians' circles, but had already fallen into the public domain and become part of the common knowledge. The field of medicine experienced hardly any gains in the New World during the sixteenth, seventeenth, and eighteenth centuries. From then on, progress within this field in Europe started flowing to South America, where such new acquisitions were restricted to a small number of professionals, whose practices were almost always limited to the main cities. In the countryside there continued to be a lack of physicians, while the ancient precepts on nutritional health still survived. This sort of scientific backwardness carried on during the republican period and even until the early twentieth century, even though modernization had already started to take place as a result of the urban-development boom of the first half of that century. The lack of physicians left the field clear for folk healers or curious people who continued to empirically put the ancient knowledge into practice, unaware of the breakthroughs of contemporary medicine.

There are written and oral records of the curative and preventive methods applied by such folk healers or, in some cases, physicians, dating back to colonial times, as well as some printed material of republican times and of the present. An example would be the works written by Leo Manfred under the titles *300 plantas medicinales argentinas* and *600 plantas medici-*

nales argentinas y sudamericanas,[1] which came out by the middle of the twentieth century.

Among the ancient traditions there is a kind of disease etiology that refers to diet disorders as a main cause for illness. An example of such disorders would be the nonobservance of the ancient principles that classified foods and beverages into cold and hot. According to this lore, health is not only maintained by avoiding consuming too many of either one of the two types and by combining them in the appropriate way; it is also deemed important to take into consideration the body's condition when food is to be consumed, avoiding, for example, taking cold foods right after hard work or exercise. Another extremely important issue, according to tradition, is the consideration of the time of the day when foods are consumed. There are some that should be eaten in the morning, for example, as they can be of less benefit if consumed at noon and even harmful if eaten at night. This would be the case of fruits, which according to the old saying are considered "Gold in the morning, silver at noon, and at night, boom!"[2] The body's functions are also of key significance, which is the reason why certain foods are not consumed during menstruation, pregnancy, the postbirth period, and recovery conditions. If a person has a fever, for example, he or she is told not to consume any foods hot in temperature or foods that can irritate the stomach, so as not to worsen the condition. Other beliefs hold that the combination of certain foods can be harmful, like that of acidic fruits and milk, which may supposedly lead to serious digestion disorders. The fact that the ancient precepts of Greco-Roman times on food classification have survived until the present in Latin America is one of the points made by George M. Foster in his study *Culture and Conquest*, a work about the European legacy transferred by the conquerors to Latin America.[3]

Indian and African Botanical-Medicinal Heritage

Many people associate South American Indians nowadays with the pictures of tribes from Amazonia. Such an image of human beings often looking weak and gaunt would suggest that the natives' diet had always been a poor one from a nutritional point of view. However, this was not always the case. If the contemporary documents on the conquest, and especially the records of the first contacts between Europeans and South Americans, are taken into consideration, such an opinion would immediately be deemed false. The relationships that resulted from the Columbian encounter of civilizations and the chronicles from the sixteenth century often depicted the Indians as healthy people with robust constitutions who were, most of the time, particularly beautiful. Their fresh skin, shiny hair, good teeth, longevity, and the ease with which native women gave birth are all factors that suggest, on the basis of current research on nutrition, that their diet was balanced and aimed to meet their particular needs. This original panorama changed very soon with the domination of the Europeans and the consequent extermination of large numbers of natives by means of simple elimination, the transmission of diseases that did not previously exist in the continent, the changes made to the land-farming system, and the diet itself. Of course, and just like any other human civilization, South American natives did not enjoy perfect health conditions during pre-Columbian times. They suffered from a number of illnesses and therefore invented formulas to treat them.

As the Europeans started to become familiar with the culture of South American Indians, they found that the natives possessed a botanical and medical knowledge that was completely different from theirs. At first, such knowledge was only in the hands of the priests and witch doctors or *piaches*, so Europeans considered it the devil's doing and fought against it, as well as against the other religious practices of the Indians. However, some curious chroniclers and certain missionaries, who also wrote some stories, showed an interest in these healing practices, which they described in their writings, but not before referring to them as heathen matters. They also started to register the names of many of the plants native to the New World, indicating the therapeutic properties they featured according to the Indian lore. The interest in this new "medicinal material" grew with time, as many of these medicines made with plants proved to be effective. During the lengthy cultural-mixing process, the European and Indian medical lore merged, giving rise to a type of knowledge that can be called *criollo*, as it came to life in the South American continent. As a result of the lack of physicians, many of these plant medicines, known as "medicinal material" and dating back to pre-Columbian times, were used, and many of the witch doctors who practiced medicine not only during colonial, but also during republican times, have been of Indian origin. Even though most of the knowledge they possessed was transmitted orally, it was also possible for it to survive, thanks to the publication of several books in the early nineteenth century, which turned out to be very popular. One of the most prominent examples of these publications is perhaps the book written by Venezuelan Gerónimo Pompa (1810–80) under the title *Colección de medicamentos indígenas*, whose first edition was printed in Puerto Cabello, Venezuela, in 1868; since then other editions of the book have been published, not only in Caracas, but also in other cities of the world, at least until 1988.

Throughout South America there are stands selling medicinal plants, both in public markets of cities and towns and in specialty stores. Such stores are commonly known as *yerbaterías* and are very much frequented by the people, as the tradition of using medicinal plants still plays a very important role in the continent. In contemporary times, especially since the 1980s, scientists have shown an ever-growing interest in the medicinal plants the Indians have used for time immemorial. The scientists have obtained many of them and analyzed them in their laboratories, recognized the effectiveness of such plants to treat sick people, and enhanced the modern pharmaceutical repertoire by including such medicinal plants. Today, the so-called naturist products are sold throughout the region in special stores or drugstores. The products offered to the public have undergone careful harvesting and treatment to allow for the preservation of their healing properties.

Among this repertoire of medicinal plants, a number are used to heal or treat certain digestion disorders, especially in rural areas. For example, severe stomach pains are treated with great mullein (*Jacquinia barbasco*), coffee senna (*Cassia occidentalis*), otoba (*Dialyanthera otoba*), *suelda con suelda* (*Commelina nudiflora*), and *tusilla* or *contrayerva* (*Dorstenia contrajerva*); when people have worms, they use papaya (*Carica papaya*) or worm bush (*Spigelia anthelmia*); for intestinal obstructions, there is the copaiba (*Copaifera officinalis*) and the *cusparia* bark (*Cusparia trifoliata*); as a purgative, there is the sand-box tree (*Hura crepitans*), the *maya* (*Bromelia chrysantha*), the physic nut (*Jatropha curcas*), and the bellyache bush (*Jatropha gossypifolia*); and as an invigorating agent, people use coca leaves (*Erythroxylum coca*).

The African people that were taken to the New World as slaves also possessed medical knowledge. They were aware of the healing properties of many plants, some of which they managed to bring with them to the Americas; others were transplanted by the very slave traders, thinking it would be advisable to have within reach anything that would be good for their "merchandise." Regarding the diet of these slaves, there are some experts who say that what they used to eat in the plantations or in any other establishments of the American continent was a much better diet than the one they enjoyed in their land of origin, where there was no guarantee that they would eat every day or even consistently, and where the meals are said to have been protein-deficient. The slave masters were the first to be interested in keeping them in good shape in this new environment, so they made sure that the slaves received meals that were appropriate, to enable them to carry out the hard labor forced upon them every day. Compared with the situation in the Caribbean Antilles, in the South American mainland the slaves were much freer, to a certain extent, and mainly used their free time to carry out subsistence farming in small land lots the owners of the haciendas would let them have.

In the mainland, slaves took care of their own sustenance, facing the problem of not having certain foods available as a result of the geographical location they were now placed in. They could not find any sorghum or millet, but they had corn and cassava, with which they were probably already familiar. They could easily get yams, rice, and plantains, as well as meat (beef, goat, pork, and poultry). The type of agriculture they practiced in their sown fields reinforced the one carried out by the South American natives in their small production units or *conucos*. These small-holding practices even exist today.

As part of their cultural memories, the Africans arriving in South America were bearers of certain knowledge on medicinal plants, which served to reinforce the medicinal material that would then make up the lore of the *sociedad criolla*, to which they were part of by means of the mixing process. One of the most significant examples of the African contribution in terms of medicinal plants was probably the use of *quimbombô* (*Hibiscus esculentus* L.). This member of the *Malvaceae* family, native to the African continent, has also received the names gumbo and okra. Special soups are prepared with the flower buds and the unripe fruits of this plant, as they are said to be very good for digestion, while its mucilaginous leaves are used to make emollient poultices.

The Arrival of Nutritional Sciences

People's concern for nutrition is relatively long-standing in South America. It was recorded in the late 1820s by hygiene manuals made for family use (private hygiene) or community use (public hygiene). These treatises or manuals written for the general public classified the foods into different categories, described the digestive process, and then pointed out certain rules that had to be followed in order to maintain good health, specifying the diets that would best suit people depending on their age or the type of work they performed. An early example of this kind of book is the one known as *Elementos de Hijiene*, written by José Félix Melizalde and published in Bogotá in 1828. He was a university professor in Bogotá who had specialized in that issue. The work is very singular and difficult to find in libraries. It dwells on the foods that make up the diet of that specific region, pointing out their characteristics and their influence on people's health. In that same century, other works were also published on the issue of hygiene, like the one by Adolfo Brunel under the title *Consideraciones sobre higiene y observaciones relativas a la de Montevideo*, published in Uruguay's capital city in 1862, or the one written by Emilio Coni, namely *Código de Higiene y Medicina Legal de la República Argentina*, published in Buenos Aires in 1891. There were also books focusing on the diet issue, such as *Tratado de la Alimentación*, by Manuel A. Diez, published in Caracas in 1896, which gives a detailed account of the nutritional values of food. All of these works captured nutritional practices and concepts that are still maintained in many rural communities today.

Yet it was not until the twentieth century that more modern handbooks started to come out and that the national governments showed an interest in peoples' nutrition. By midcentury, the health departments of many South American governments started to create offices devoted to the study of the diet issue and to achieve improvements on nutritional matters at the national level, while independent institutes also emerged to serve this same purpose. The first of these bodies to come to life was the Instituto de Nutrición de Argentina, which was founded in 1928 by nutritionist Pedro Escudero. To a great extent, such an inrush of nutrition into the institutions of the South American governments was a consequence of the work carried out by the Food and Agriculture Organization (FAO), founded in 1945. This international body created projects for Latin America, which began to be implemented in 1949, when the first meetings of Rio de Janeiro and Lima took place, and then through the ones held in Santiago de Chile (1950) and Buenos Aires (1952).[4] The FAO initiatives paved the way for the creation of a number of independent institutes in the continent devoted to nutritional matters. These would be some of the most important facts related to the establishment of food science in South America.

The institutions that have survived until the present have been facing ever-intensifying problems within their areas of responsibility. They are challenged not only by the need to combat the traditional lore on the nutritional values or harmful nature of the different foods, but also by people's diet disorders. The accelerated increase of the population and the periodic economic crises suffered by the South American countries have brought about an increment in the number of people with very few means of support and the subsequent high malnutrition levels, which constitutes one of the headaches of government leaders in the continent. In an attempt to fight the hunger problem looming over the regional public-health scene, many programs aimed at improving the standard of living of most South Americans have been implemented, some of them more successful than others.

MODERN NUTRITION

The Discussion on the Caloric Requirements

In the twentieth century, the issue of people's caloric requirements was addressed by a large number of scientific publications. Particularly worth mentioning is the contribution of some South American specialists, among which the works of the Brazilian professor Josué de Castro on this topic have played a key role, one of the most important being his *Geografía do fame*, which has been translated into several languages and which drew the attention of the international community to the nutritional problems of the tropical countries.[5] In another one of his works, Castro points out that even though the food needs of human beings are basically equal with regard to "the energy requirements needed to maintain the innate heat and to be able to perform the different physiological tasks, as well as the need to be provided with the different nutrients: proteins, carbohydrates, fat, mineral salts and vitamins," they are not equal in quantitative terms, as the climate is determinant of humans' lifestyle—making a difference in the quantity of nutrients demanded by the body—as well as of their energy outputs.[6] According to the author, the geological and climatic conditions of a specific zone not only determine the protein levels needed by the human body, but also affect the chemical composition of the soil and, therefore, the food.

Castro based his studies on the already accepted premise that the numbers calculated for temperate zones cannot be applied as universal patterns. His experiments—aimed at creating a diet that would help provide an energy balance to the human organism—focused on the calculation of two basic values: first, the energy output of living organisms in the tropical lands, and second, the energy potential of foods.

The human body is not a simple thermometer that registers the changes in temperature. It actually shows physiological reactions when such variations occur. Thus, the intensity of the work carried out by the people in the tropics and their energy requirements can vary. One of the main conclusions stated by the author once he has described his experiments in detail is that the working capacity in the tropical lands is lower than in the temperate zones:

In equatorial, tropical and subtropical zones—with hot climate and relative humidity levels—the intensity of work is lower than in areas with mild or cold climates. Besides, we had already found out, empirically, that the work done in the tropical colonies is less productive than the one done in the European countries, and that in the former workers are not able to do eight kilogram-meters medium work per second, as is the case in the latter. As the amount of energy consumed during work is in direct proportion to the number of kilogram-meters done, the amount of energy has to be also lower in the tropical zones.[7]

Food is what, in the end, wholly offsets the energy loss of humans, with the organic foods (proteins, fat, and carbohydrates) making up their "energy potential." In this sense, as the caloric requirements are mainly provided by the organic foods, the author formulated a number of conclusions on the portions human beings in the tropical areas should consume from each food category.

As Castro concluded, "in the tropical regions, we must be moderate, avoid consuming too many proteins, while being careful to not have less than the minimum needed to attain a nutritional balance. The average proportion of one gram per kilo (weight), i.e. 70 grams daily, is reasonable, provided that around 50 per cent is made up by whole proteins."[8] He states that, in tropical climates, a high level of protein consumption can lead to an increment in combustion and, thus, in metabolism, which would make it even more difficult for human beings to acclimatize to the tropical lands. Conversely, a low consumption rate of proteins may result in developmental problems that are shown in the short stature of many groups of people. Another effect of low protein consumption is the generation of edemas in the tissues and the consequent increase in weight. The edemas appear due to the lack of globulin and serine in the blood, making people look healthier because of their high body weight, whereas other people with no protein deficit feature a lower body weight.

As for carbohydrates, Castro explains that they make up 50 to 70 percent of the total energy of normal diets, although the diet of mainly poor people from the tropical regions contains up to 80 to 90 percent of carbohydrates, which damages their health. In this sense, Castro gives the people from the tropical regions two basic pieces of advice: first, avoid consuming carbohydrates and do not let these types of food (often the cheapest ones) be higher than two-thirds of the whole calorie consumption, and second, offset the calorie requirements with fats and proteins. In case it is not possible to consume foods from these other two groups, the author recommends reducing the calorie consumption instead of consuming carbohydrates in excess. Another important piece of advice to be followed in the tropical countries with regard to the consumption of carbohydrates is, according to Castro, that some of them to be consumed include fruits, unwashed rice, oats, and wheat grain, and not only starchy flours or tubers. He also recommends being careful with the types of methods used to cook starchy foods, avoiding the European methods and instead applying those from certain "primitive" peoples.

The third group of foods that provides the human body with calories is fat. The author recommends a daily fat consumption of around 30 grams in the form of milk, butter, certain vegetable oils, and fish. This advice is based on the fact that "the hot climate diminishes the intensity of the digestive processes and hinders the proper functioning of the liver, which suggests that a diet very rich in fats could irritate the digestive system or increase the possibilities of liver failure."[9] Castro explains that his statements are not intended to change the diets of those peoples who are far from fulfilling such recommendations, as is the case of Bahian cuisine from northeastern Brazil, which is characterized by an excessive intake of *dendé* (palm oil).

Castro's calculations are based on the general climatic conditions of the tropical zones, but these obviously vary from one country to another within this region, which calls for the need to adjust the figures obtained.

Recently published data in table 7.1 give an account of the average daily calorie intake per inhabitant in the region.

It is very probable that the nutritional panorama depicted by these data has varied, worsening the situation in South American countries. This in turn means the gap between the numbers presented for the United States and those of the South America may have widened.

What the Data Suggest: Is the Staple Diet Balanced and Rich in Nutrients?

It is particularly difficult to draw any conclusion about the real nutritional condition of the South American peoples. Despite the efforts made by nutritionists and governments in the region, statistics are not produced on a regular basis in every country, and the criteria used differ throughout the region. Dietary surveys have been carried out only in very recent times, and no document has been produced so far presenting a rigorous summary of their results. Therefore, the analyses have to be based on official statistics, which are not reliable enough, as the data they offer are often different from those obtained through surveys conducted by private firms.

The general characteristics of the typical South American diet will now be presented, based on a summary analysis of the nutritional values of the traditional South American foods.

Table 7.1
Dietary Outlook in South America

Country	Calories Daily average calorie input per inhabitant (1997)	Undernourishment Percentage of rachitic children (1990–1997)	Overfeeding		Percentage of diabetics (2000)
			Mortality rate from coronary diseases per 100,000 inhabitants (latest available data)		
			men	women	
Argentina	3,093	--	127.66	35.13	3.60%
Bolivia	2,174	16	–	–	2.10%
Brazil	2,974	6	415.42	205.80	2.90%
Colombia	2,597	8	173.03	100.02	2.60%
Chile	2,796	1	122.60	49.71	3.50%
Ecuador	2,679	17	38.86	19.82	2.30%
Guyana	2,530	12	203.65	108.20	3.40%
Paraguay	2,566	4	259.30	128.02	2.00%
Peru	2,302	8	38.21	18.09	2.60%
Suriname	2,665	--	250.47	125.78	3.30%
Uruguay	2,816	5	181.20	65.65	3.70%
Venezuela	2,321	5	227.05	111.53	2.80%
Totals	31,513	82	2,037.45	967.75	34.8%
United States	3,699	1	192.49	77.23	4.80%

Source: Erik Millstone and Tim Lang, Atlas de l'alimentation dans le monde (Paris: FAO, 2003), pp. 112–19, 128.

High Consumption of Carbohydrates

The high carbohydrate intake is not only due to the very important role played by sugar in the daily diet, but also to the high proportion of carbohydrates in some foods such as potatoes, onions, rice, or peas, among others, which are usually used to prepare the typical dishes in the continent. Another important factor that contributes to the high carbohydrate intake is the significant consumption of refreshing beverages—most of them sweetened—such as sodas or fruit juices. The special love of beer accounts for the big abdomens of many South Americans, often believed to be a sign of good nutrition, which is not always the case. In Venezuela, this abdomen protuberance is called barriguita cervecera (beer belly).

Significant Proportion of Proteins

South Americans have traditionally considered meat (especially beef) to be an essential ingredient of their diet. This trend is particularly seen in the meat-producing countries Venezuela, Colombia, Brazil, Uruguay, and especially Argentina. Despite the high prices of this product, the South

American governments have always tried to adopt measures aimed at reducing the cost, while the people make every effort to be able to buy it.

Importance of Fats

The consumption of animal fats, such as beef fat or lard, is nowadays
relatively lower than in the past, as vegetable fats—like peanut, corn, and
soy oils, among others—have been used to replace them. Nevertheless,
the typical South American diet still features a high intake of lipids. Fat
is used for the preparation of almost all the typical dishes from the various
gastronomical zones of the region, starting with the *sofrito*, which is the
basic sauce of a great number of dishes in South America.

Significant Intake of Vitamins C and A

There is a significant proportion of vitamins C and A in two of the basic
ingredients of the continental diet, namely chilies and plantains. Chili
peppers are widely known for their high levels of vitamin C, which is also
found in some fruits like guava or citruses—commonly consumed fresh in
the form of juices or *batidos* (shakes). Plantains are rich in vitamin A, the
content of which remarkably increases when the fruit is cooked.

NOTES

1. These two works were updated by their author and combined to create a
single work: Leo Manfred, *Siete mil recetas botánicas a base de mil trescientas plantas
medicinales* (Buenos Aires: Editorial Kier, 1947).
2. "Por la mañana oro, al mediodía plata y por la noche matan."
3. George McClelland Foster, *Culture and Conquest: America's Spanish Heritage*
(Chicago: Quadrangle Books, 1960), pp. 14ff. The study of this matter was presented by this same author in a monograph under the title "Hippocrates' Latin
American Legacy: Hot and Cold in Contemporary Folk Medicine," in *Colloquia
in Anthropology* vol. 2, ed. R. K. Wetherington (Dallas: Southern Methodist University and Fort Burgwin Research Center, 1978), pp. 3–19.
4. Gove Hambidge, *The Story of FAO* (New York: D. Van Nostrand, 1955), p.
179ff.
5. This work was translated and published in English as Josué de Castro, *The
Geography of Hunger* (Boston: Little, Brown, 1952).
6. Josué de Castro, *La alimentación en los trópicos* (Mexico City: Fondo de Cultura Económica, 1946), p. 10.
7. Ibid., pp. 56–57.
8. Ibid., p. 75.
9. Ibid., p. 86.

Glossary

ajicero Hot sauce (usually homemade), prepared with hot peppers, vinegar, and spices. It is also the name given to the container of such sauce.

arepa A native bread of Venezuela and Colombia.

arroz Rice.

asado Roast.

atol, atole Beverage that is generally prepared with cooked corn, water, and other ingredients. In South America, this word is also used to mean "beverage" in general.

barbacoa Barbecue.

buchada The entrails of edible animals.

cachiri Fermented *casabe* beverage prepared by Indians.

cafecito Cup of coffee.

carato Refreshing beverage prepared with water, sugar, and the pulp of a certain fruit.

catibía Grated, pressed, and squeezed cassava pulp.

cena Dinner.

charqui Salted and dried meat.

chicha Native beverage with corn base.

choclo Fresh corn.

chupe   Soup similar to chowders.

cocuy   Name used in Venezuela to designate the plant known in other parts of the continent as *ágave* (*Agave Americana* L.), which is used in Mexico to prepare *pulque*. The term is also used to designate the liquor extracted from this plant.

criollo, criolla   Those born in the New World who are descendants of Europeans or Africans. By extension, the term is also used to refer to the societies that result from a mixing process, as well as to the plants and animals that are native to Latin America or that have acclimatized in the region.

dendé   Palm oil.

desayuno   Breakfast.

dulce   Unrefined sugar.

empanada   Wheat pastry with different fillings.

ensalada   Salad.

feria   Celebration.

frijoles or frisoles   Beans.

gaucho   Cattle herder of the Argentine Pampas.

hacienda   Plantation.

llanero   Cattle herder of the Colombian and Venezuelan Llanos.

manioc   Tuber whose scientific name is *Manihot esculenta* Crantz, equivalent to *mandioca* (tapioca) and *yuca* (cassava). It is widely used in South America and especially in the Amazonian zone.

mate   Bitter and greenish infusion or tea made from the leaves of a tree native to South America.

orixá   A saint from the Afro-Brazilian tradition.

pisillo   Dish prepared with meat, which is salted and then desalted, shredded, and fried or roasted with different seasonings.

sofrito   Basic sauce for a number of dishes.

sopa   Soup.

Resource Guide

BOOKS

Antúnez de Mayolo, Santiago. *La nutrición en el Antiguo Perú*. Lima: Banco Central de Reserva del Perú, 1985.

Bacon, Josephine. *The Complete Guide to Exotic Fruits and Vegetables*. London: Xanadu, 1988.

Cascudo, Luís da Câmara. *História da Alimentação no Brasil*. Belo Horizonte, Brazil: Ediçoes Itatiaia, 1983.

Castro, Josué de. *The Geography of Hunger*. Boston: Little, Brown, 1952.

———. *La alimentación en los trópicos*. Mexico City: Fondo de Cultura Económica, 1946.

Coe, Sophie. *America's First Cuisines*. Austin: University of Texas Press, 1994.

———. "Inca Food: Animal and Mineral." In *Petits Propos Culinaires*, vol. 29, 7–17. London: Prospect Books, 1988.

Coe, Sophie, and Michael Coe. *The True History of Chocolate*. London: Thames and Hudson, 1996.

Crosby, Alfred W., Jr. *The Columbian Exchange*. Westport, Conn.: Greenwood Press, 1972.

Fernández-Armesto, Felipe. *Food: A History*. Oxford: Macmillan, 2001.

Foster, Nelson, and Linda S. Cordell. *Chilies to Chocolate: Food the Americas Gave the World*. Tucson: University of Arizona Press, 1992.

Freeling, M., and Virginia Walbot, eds. *The Maize Handbook*. New York: Springer-Verlag, 1994.

Gosden, Chris, and Jon Hather. *The Prehistory of Food: Appetites for Change*. New York: Routledge, 1999.

Gutarra Carhuamaca, Jesús y León Valderrama. *Pachamanca: El festín terrenal/The Earthy Feast*. Lima: Universidad San Martín de Porres, 2001.

Hambidge, Gove. *The Story of FAO*. New York: D. Van Nostrand, 1955.

Horton, D. E., and H. Fano. *Potato Atlas/Atlas de la Pomme de Terre/Atlas de la Papa*. Lima: Centro Internacional de la Papa, 1985.

Jennings, Jesse D., and Edward Norbeck, eds. *Prehistoric Man in the New World*. Chicago: University of Chicago Press, 1964.

Keller, Carlos. *Revolución en la agricultura*. Santiago de Chile: Editorial Zig-Zag, 1956.

Krickeberg, Walter, et al. *Pre-Columbian American Religions*. New York: Holt, Rinehart and Winston, 1969.

Lee, Richard, and Irven Devore, eds. *Man the Hunter*. Chicago: Aldine, 1968.

Lima, Claudia. *Tachos e Panelas: Historiografia da alimentação brasileira*. Recife, Brazil: Editora Comunicarte, 1999.

Patiño, Víctor Manuel. *Historia de la cultura material en la América Equinoccial*. Bogotá: Biblioteca de la Presidencia de la República, 1984.

Ramos, Arthur. *Las culturas negras en el Nuevo Mundo*. Mexico City: Fondo de Cultura Económica, 1943.

Roosevelt, Anna Curtenius. *Parmana: Prehistoric Maize and Manioc Subsistence along the Amazon and Orinoco*. New York: Academic Press, 1980.

Salaman, Redcliffe. *The History and Social Influence of the Potato*. Cambridge: Cambridge University Press, 1985.

Sánchez Albornoz, Nicolás. *La población de América Latina desde los tiempos precolombinos al año 2000*. Madrid: Alianza Editorial, 1973.

Storni, Julio. *Bromatología indígena: Solución precolombiana al problema alimenticio*. Tucumán, Argentina: Universidad de Tucumán, 1942.

Super, John C. *Food, Conquest, and Colonization in Sixteenth-Century Spanish America*. Albuquerque: University of New Mexico Press, 1988.

Super, John C., and Thomas Wright. *Food, Politics, and Society in Latin America*. Lincoln: University of Nebraska Press, 1985.

Thomas, Hugh. *The Slave Trade: The History of the Atlantic Slave Trade 1440–1870*. New York: Simon and Schuster, 1997.

Vélez Boza, Fermín y Graciela Valery de Vélez. *Plantas alimenticias de Venezuela*. Caracas: Fundación Bigott, Sociedad de Ciencias Naturales La Salle, 1990.

Viola, Herman J., and Carolyn Margolis. *Seeds of Change*. Washington, D.C.: Smithsonian Institution Press, 1991.

Wesley Cowan, C., and Patty Jo Watson, eds. *The Origins of Agriculture: An International Perspective*. Washington, D.C.: Smithsonian Institution Press, 1992.

Woolfe, J. A., with S. V. Poats. *The Potato in the Human Diet*. New York: Cambridge University Press, 1987.

COOKBOOKS

General

Bensusan, Susan. *Latin American Cooking: A Treasury of Recipes from the South American Countries, Mexico and the Caribbean*. New York: Galahad Books, 1974.

Leonard, Jonathan Norton. *Latin American Cooking*. New York: Time-Life Books, 1968.

Ortiz, Elisabeth Lambert. *The Book of Latin American Cooking*. New York: Alfred A. Knopf, 1979.

Argentina

Brooks, Shirley Lomax, *Argentina Cooks: Treasured Recipes from the Nine Regions of Argentina*. New York: Hippocrene, 2003.

Gandulfo, Petrona. *El libro de Doña Petrona*. Buenos Aires: Talleres Gráficos de la Compañía General Fabril Financiera, 1940.

Gran libro de la cocina argentina. Buenos Aires: Emecé, 1991.

Bolivia

Paredes Candia, Antonio. *La comida popular boliviana*. La Paz: Edición de Antonio Paredes Candia, 1990.

Sierra de Méndez, Lola. *Cocina típica regional boliviana*. La Paz: Ministerio de Educación; Dirección de Antropología, 1963.

Brazil

Andrade, Margarette de. *Brazilian Cookery: Traditional and Modern*. Rio de Janeiro: A Casa do Livro Eldorado, 1985.

Bateman, M., et al. *Cafe Brazil*. New York: McGraw-Hill, 1999.

Botafogo, Dolores. *The Art of Brazilian Cookery*. New York: Hippocrene, 1993.

Fernandes, Caloca. *Viagem gastronômica através do Brasil*. São Paulo: Editora Senac, 2001.

Idone, Christopher. *Brazil: A Cook's Tour*. New York: Clarkson Potter, 1995.

O prato nosso de cada dia: Arte culinária brasileira. São Paulo: Editora Yucas, 1993.

Vianna, Hildegardes. *A cozinha baiana: Seu folclore, suas receitas*. São Paulo: Ediçoes GDR, 1987.

Chile

Eyzaguirre Lyon, Hernán. *Sabor y saber de la cocina chilena*. Santiago de Chile: Andrés Bello, 1987.

Joelson, Daniel. *Tasting Chile: A Celebration of Authentic Chilean Foods and Wines*. New York: Hippocrene, 2004.

Merino, Augusto [Ruperto de Nola]. *Cocina chilena familiar*. Santiago, Chile: Editorial Sudamericana, 1998.

Colombia

Gran libro de la cocina colombiana. Bogotá: Círculo de Lectores, 1984.

McCausland-Gallo, Patricia. *Secrets of Colombian Cooking*. New York: Hippocrene, 2004.

Montaña, Antonio. *El sabor de Colombia*. Bogotá: Villegas Editores, 1994.

Ecuador

Gran libro de la cocina ecuatoriana. Quito: Círculo de Lectores, n.d.

French Guiana

Horth, Régine. *La Guyane gastronomique et traditionnelle*. Paris: Éditions Caribéennes, 1988.

Guyana

Seeraj, Sandra. *Made in Guyana*. N.p.: Ministry of Information, 1980.

Paraguay

Livieres de Artecona, Raquel. *La cocinera paraguaya*. Asunción: La Colmena, 1931.

Velilla de Aquino, Josefina. *Tembi'u paraguai: Comida paraguaya*. Asunción: RP Ediciones, 1987.

Peru

Hinostroza de Molina, Gloria, et al. *Cocinas regionales peruanas*. Lima: Universidad San Martín de Porres, Escuela Profesional de Turismo y Hotelería, 1999.

Sanbury Aguirre, Jorge. *La Gran Cocina Peruana*. Lima: Peru Reporting, 1995.

Sison Porras de De La Guerra, Josie. *El Perú y sus manjares: Un crisol de culturas*. Lima: Edición de Josie Sison Porras de De la Guerra, 1994.

Suriname

John, Yvonne. *Guyanese Seed of Vegetables, Seafood, and Desserts*. Holly Hill: K&M, 1985.

Uruguay

Dumont, M. *El gorro blanco*. Montevideo: Casa A. Barreiro y Ramos, 1946.

Venezuela

Scannone, Armando. *Mi cocina*. Caracas: Armando Scannone, 1982.
————. *Mi cocina II*. Caracas: Armando Scannone, 1994.

WEB SITES

General

Carnegie Library of Pittsburgh. "Latin American Food & Cooking." http://www.carnegielibrary.org/subject/food/latin.html.
English Spanish Link.com. "Spanish Recipe. Spanish Food...Food Products Spain/Recetas de Cocina en Inglés y Español..." http://www.englishspanishlink.com/recipes.htm.
GlobalCilk S. L. "Colección de Recetas de Cocina Sudamericana." http://www.cocinadelmundo.com/continentes/south_america.html.
Gupo IDA S. L. "El Portal de Recetas del Mundo." http://www.arecetas.com/america.
Hamre, Bonnie. "South America for Visitors." http://gosouthamerica.about.com.

Argentina

Cicarelli, José. "Argentina Recipes." http://orbita.starmedia.com/~recipes_to_collect/.
GARDEL server. "Todo sobre la Cocina Argentina." http://argentina.informatik.uni-muenchen.de/recetas/.

Bolivia

Bolivia Web. "Recipes Gallery-Traditional Bolivian Cooking." http://www.boliviaweb.com/recipes/english/index.htm.

Brazil

Duro, Elton. "CookBrazil: Brazilian Food Recipes." http://www.cookbrazil.com/.
Polasky, Rod. "Brazilian Cooking: Anthropology of Food." http://www.archaeo
    link.com/brazilian_cooking_anthropology_o.htm.
Thomson, Sheila. "Maria's Cookbook." http://www.maria-brazil.org/fdind.htm.

Chile

Canfield, Eric. "Chilean Food." http://www.geocities.com/TheTropics/Cabana/
    6234/food.htm.
CFFA. "The World of Chilean Fresh Fruit." http://www.cffausa.org/m_recipes.
    htm.

Colombia

Comidacolombiana.com. http://www.comidacolombiana.com/guia.htm.
Universidad de Los Andes. "Comidas Típicas de Colombia." http://www.uniandes.
    edu.co/Colombia/Recetas/recetas.html.

Guyana

Moses, Wayne. "Guyana Outpost: Wayne's Guyana Page." http://guyana.gweb
    works.com/recipes/recipes_cat.shtml.

Paraguay

Weinstock, Steven D. "Paraguayan Recipes." http://www.pyadopt.org/recipe.
    html.

Peru

ServerPro. "Peru Recipes at Food Down Under Recipe Database." http://food
    downunder.com/cgi-bin/search.cgi?q=peru.
Yanuq Inc. "Yanuq Cooking in Peru." http://www.cocinaperuana.com/english/.

Suriname

TROPILAB INC. "Recipes from the Surinam Kitchen." http://www.tropilab.
    com/surinamkitchen.html.

Uruguay

Domenech, Enrique. "Recetas de Uruguay-Receta Cocina Uruguaya." http://
www.kike.c.telefonica.net/endosan/uruguay.htm#Carbonada%20criolla.
Gupo IDA S. L. "A Recetas de Uruguay." http://www.arecetas.com/uruguay/.

Venezuela

Cantv. "Cantv Páginas Amarillas: Guía Gastronómica." http://www.paginas
amarillascantv.com.ve/gastronomia/default.asp.
Centro de Estudios Gastronómicos de Venezuela. "CEGA." http://cega.org.ve.
Scannone, Armando. "El Placer de Comer." http://www.elplacerdecomer.com/.

Bibliography

Acosta, Joseph de. *Historia natural y moral de las Indias*. 1590. Reprint, Madrid: Ramón Anglés, 1894.

Alfaro, Alfonso. "Los espacios de la sazón." In *Congreso sobre Patrimonio Gastronómico y Turismo Cultural en América Latina y el Caribe*, vol. 1:1, 55–68. Mexico City: CONACULTA, 2002.

Brack Egg, Antonio. *Frutas del Perú*. Lima: Universidad San Martín de Porres, 2003.

Briz Garizurleta, Marcela. "Los restaurantes ante la modernidad." In *Cuarto Congreso sobre Patrimonio Gastronómico y Turismo Cultural en América Latina y el Caribe*, 197–200. Mexico City: CONACULTA, 2003.

Cámara Cascudo, Luis da. *Diccionário do folclore brasileiro*. Rio de Janeiro: Istituto Nacional do Livro, 1954.

Carvalho-Neto, Paulo de. *Diccionario del folklore ecuatoriano*. Quito: Editorial Casa de la Cultura Ecuatoriana, 1964.

———. *Historia del folklore iberoamericano*. Santiago de Chile: Editorial Universitaria, 1969.

Castillo de Lucas, Antonio. *Refranerillo de la alimentación*. Madrid: Gráficas Reunidas, S.A., 1940.

Castro, Josué de. *The Geography of Hunger*. Boston: Little, Brown, 1952.

———. *La alimentación en los trópicos*. Mexico City: Fondo de Cultura Económica, 1946.

Cervantes, Abdiel. "Los jóvenes en las cocinas." In *Cuarto Congreso sobre Patrimonio Gastronómico y Turismo Cultural en América Latina y el Caribe. (Memorias)*, 27–30. Mexico City: CONACULTA, 2003.

Coluccio, Félix. *Diccionario folklórico argentino*. Buenos Aires: Librería El Ateneo Editorial, 1950.

Deleito y Piñuela, José. *La mujer, la casa y la moda*. Madrid: Espasa Calpe, 1946.

Domingo, Xavier. *De la olla al mole*. Madrid: Ediciones Cultura Hispánica, 1984.

Foster, George McClelland. *Culture and Conquest: America's Spanish Heritage*. Chicago: Quadrangle Books, 1960.

———. "Hippocrates' Latin American Legacy—Hot and Cold in Contemporary Folk Medicine." In *Colloquia in Anthropology* vol. 2, ed. R.K. Wetherington, 3–19. Dallas: Southern Methodist University and Fort Burgwin Research Center, 1978.

Furlong, Guillermo. *Historia social y cultural del Río de la Plata*. Buenos Aires: Tipográfica Editora Argentina, 1969.

Hambidge, Gove. *The Story of FAO*. New York: D. Van Nostrand, 1955.

Lovera, José Rafael. *Historia de la alimentación en Venezuela*. Caracas: Centro de Estudios Gastronómicos, 1998.

———. *Manuel Guevara Vasconcelos o la política del convite*. Caracas: Academia Nacional de la Historia, 1998.

Manfed, Leo. *Siete mil recetas botánicas a base de mil trescientas plantas medicinales*. Buenos Aires: Editorial Kier, 1947.

Millstone, Erik, and Tim Lang. *Atlas de l'alimentation dans le monde*. Paris: FAO, 2003.

Moreno, Victor A. "Los jóvenes y la cocina en Venezuela." In *Cuarto Congreso sobre Patrimonio Gastronómico y Turismo Cultural en América Latina y el Caribe*. (*Memorias*), 19–26. Mexico City: CONACULTA, 2003.

Mösbach, Ernesto Wilhelm de. *Botánica indígena de Chile*. Santiago de Chile: Museo Chileno de Arte Precolombino, Fundación Andes, Editorial Andrés Bello, 1992.

Nuix y Perpiñá, José. *Reflexiones imparciales sobre la humanidad de los españoles en las Indias*. 1780. Reprint, Madrid: Ediciones Atlas, 1944.

O'Leary, Simón B., ed. *Memorias del General O'Leary publicadas por su hijo*. Vol. 24. Caracas: Imprenta de El Monitor, 1884.

Patiño, Víctor Manuel. *Plantas cultivadas y animales domésticos en América Equinoccial*. 6 vols. Cali, Colombia: Imprenta Departamental, 1963–74.

Sánchez Botero, Esther. "Potencial y riesgo de la Gastronomía en América Latina." In *Congreso sobre Patrimonio Gastronómico y Turismo Cultural en América Latina y el Caribe*, vol. 1:2, 77–95. Mexico City: CONACULTA, 2002.

Silva, Silvestre P. *Frutas-Brasil*. São Paulo: Empresa das Artes, 1991.

Strauss K., Rafael. *Diccionario de cultura popular*. Caracas: Fundación Bigott, 1999.

Tauro, Alberto. *Diccionario enciclopédico del Perú*. 3 vols. Buenos Aires: Editorial Américalee, 1966.

The Visual Encyclopedia of Food. New York: Macmillan, 1996.

Index

About the Author

JOSÉ RAFAEL LOVERA is Associate Professor, School of History, Universidad Central de Venezuela, Caracas, and the Director of Centro de Estudios Gastronómicos (CEGA), Caracas, which trains young chefs and promotes Latin American gastronomy.